*f*P

The Path to
PURPOSE

Helping Our Children Find

Their Calling in Life

WILLIAM DAMON

FREE PRESS

New York   London   Toronto   Sydney

FREE PRESS

A Division of Simon & Schuster, Inc.
1230 Avenue of the Americas
New York, NY 10020

First Free Press hardcover edition April 2008

FREE PRESS and colophon are trademarks of Simon & Schuster, Inc.

For information about special discounts for bulk purchases, please contact
Simon & Schuster Special Sales at 1-800-456-6798 or business@simonandschuster.com.

Designed by Katy Riegel

Manufactured in the United States of America

10 9 8 7 6 5 4 3 2 1

Library of Congress Cataloging-in-Publication Data
Damon, William.
The path to purpose: helping our children find their calling in life/William Damon.
    p. cm.
  1. Conduct of life. 2. Goal (Psychology). 3. Motivation (Psychology).
  4. Self-actualization (Psychology). 5. Child rearing—Moral and ethical aspects.
  6. Life skills. I. Title.
BJ1581.2D36 2008
649'.7—dc22   2007049583

ISBN-13: 978-1-4165-3723-6
ISBN-10:   1-4165-3723-6

To the memory of Helen M. Damon

CONTENTS

Contents

PREFACE

In my career as a research psychologist, I have always chosen topics of study that seemed interesting and important to me (or why would I bother?), but I have never felt *compelled* to explore a particular subject. The idea of studying purpose came upon me differently. It did not feel like just another research topic but rather a culmination of the work that I had been doing on moral commitment, character education, and human development for over thirty years. What's more, at a time when a prevalent sense of emptiness looms as one of our greatest contemporary psychological dangers, the study of purpose seemed to me crucial in a societal sense.

In my prior work, I had encountered the notion of purpose many times, but dimly and indirectly, as if through a telescope with an ill-fitted lens. None of my earlier studies was about purpose per se; yet I now see that much of what I have been trying to understand for many years does in fact hinge on purpose. A study I conducted (with Anne Colby) of extraordinary moral commitment found that people who pursue noble purposes are filled with joy, despite the constant sacrifices that they feel called upon to make.[1] In a subsequent series of studies (with Howard Gardner and Mihaly Csikszentmihalyi) of men and women who have done socially valuable "good work" in their careers, I was struck by how vividly these people were able to answer our questions about what they were trying to accomplish and why.[2] An elevated purpose was always on their minds, driving their daily efforts. This purpose was their ultimate concern, essential to all their personal successes—it gave them energy; it gave them satisfaction when they accomplished their goals; and it gave them persistence when they ran into obstacles. Later, when I was invited to help create some educational workshops for fostering good work among mid-career journalists, I and my colleagues found that the most useful opening question for our training workshops was: "What is the purpose that you are trying to accomplish in your work?"[3]

This work led me to examine how young people find their purposes in life. Do adolescents have purposes, and if so, how do they learn them? What kinds of purposes, in addition to those related to careers, are inspiring today's young? What happens when young people are unable to find any purpose at all to devote themselves to? The present book is the first account of the insights that I and my students have been gaining through our initial research into these questions.[4]

This is the third book that I have written about youth development with a public audience in mind—one per decade, it seems, since 1988: *The Moral Child* in 1988; *Greater Expectations* in 1995; and now *The Path to Purpose*. Looking back, I can see that each book has been to some extent a product of its time. During the 1980s, I was troubled about the ethic of moral relativism that was swaying the intellectual currents of American culture and beginning to trickle down to schools and the media. In *The Moral Child*, I made a case for the universality of core moral values and the importance of clarity in the moral education of young people. A fair number of people read the book, but it certainly did not have much impact on our cultural practices. Indeed, by the 1990s, the culture of child rearing had become thoroughly dominated by approaches that looked askance at moral standards—and, for that matter, standards of any kind—as vestiges of insensitive traditionalism. Self-esteem had become the holy grail of child rearing, and parents were advised to avoid "traumatizing" their (supposedly) fragile children by asserting authority too forcefully or urging them to strive for excellence, take on challenges, and control their behavior according to ethical strictures. In response, I wrote *Greater Expectations: Overcoming the Culture of Indulgence in Our Homes and Schools*. This time, I believe, people did listen (not just to me—other like-minded social critics were voicing similar concerns). By the end of the decade, phrases such as "high standards" and "character education" could be heard on the tongues of influential educators and public officials whenever they spoke about their policies for youth. A number of things did start to improve: youth crime has abated to some extent; voluntary service among the young has skyrocketed; and most of the "experts" stopped treating self-esteem as the highest goal of human development. These, I believe, are all good developments, improving capacities to promote the well-being and future prospects of our young. And many young people today are thriving in every sense of the word.

But the present time, too, has its hazards, and they are serious.

The most pervasive problem of the day is a sense of emptiness that has ensnared many young people in long periods of drift during a time in their lives when they should be defining their aspirations and making progress toward their fulfillment. For too many young people today, apathy and anxiety have become the dominant moods, and disengagement or even cynicism has replaced the natural hopefulness of youth.

This is not a problem that can be addressed by solutions advanced in the past. In fact, the high standards that I and others have argued for are not a sufficient answer to this particular matter. The message that young people do best when they are challenged to strive, to achieve, to serve—a message that I still hold with conviction—fails to address the most essential question of all: *For what purpose?* Or, in a word, *Why?* For young people, this concern means starting to ask, and answer, questions such as: What do I hope to accomplish with all my efforts, with all the striving that I am expected to do? What are the higher goals that give these efforts meaning? What matters to me; and why should it matter? What is my ultimate concern in life? Unless we make such questions a central part of our conversations with young people, we can do little but sit back and watch while they wander into a sea of confusion, drift, self-doubt, and anxiety—feelings that too often arise when work and striving are unaccompanied by a sense of purpose.

Youth is a time of idealism, and young people take advice about seeking fulfillment and passion in life seriously. But such advice, given only at the margins of their daily experience (such as at commencement time or other ceremonial occasions), tends to be rich in generalities and sparse in useful details. In the real world of competition, job requirements, and societal responsibilities, how, the young person wonders, can I manage to find something that is both rewarding and meaningful? How can I pursue my dreams and avoid "selling out" without diminishing my chances to provide for myself and the family I would like to have? How can I earn a living as a valued member of society and make a positive difference in the world? These are questions that, sooner or later, all young people must confront in order to make their most crucial life choices.

Perhaps they find the answers in their schools or colleges? I wish I could say that this was the case. Most secondary schools are good at building basic skills, and they have been improving at this task in recent years. Colleges are good at exposing young people to a wonderful array of ideas and cultural understandings. All of these educational gifts enrich a student's intellectual and personal life in immeasurable ways. But when it comes to guiding students toward future paths that they will find rewarding and meaningful, our schools fall short. Students learn bits and pieces of knowledge that they may see little use for; and from time to time someone at a school assembly urges them to go and do great things in the world. When it comes to drawing connections between the two—that is, showing students why and how a math formula or a history lesson could be important for some purpose that a student may wish to pursue—schools too often fall far short.

If you visit a typical classroom and listen to what the teacher enjoins students to do, you will hear a host of study assignments, exam instructions, and lots of drill and practice. If you listen for the teacher's reasons *why* the students should perform these tasks, you will hear a host of narrow, instrumental goals, such as doing well in the class, getting good grades and avoiding failure, or perhaps—if the students are lucky—the value of learning a specific skill for its own sake. But rarely (if ever) will you hear the teacher discuss with students broader purposes that any of these goals might lead to. Why do people read or write poetry? Why do scientists split genes? Why, indeed, did I myself work hard to become a teacher? Incredibly, in all my years as a scholar of youth development and education, I have never seen a single instance of a teacher sharing with students the reasons why he or she went into the teaching profession. Nor, for that matter, have I often heard such conversations about the deeper meaning of our efforts within families, or in any media shows marketed to youth. How can we expect that young people will find meaning in what they are doing if we so rarely draw their attention to the personal meaning and purpose of what we work at in our daily lives?

My studies—and this book—have a purpose of their own: To make a case for the primary importance of purpose in youth development. I hope to make this case for all those who take an interest in the young, whether as parents, educators, scientists, professionals in the field of youth development, or citizens in the society that today's young will someday inherit. Among all these constituencies, the notion of purpose is already familiar to some degree. There have been some prior studies of youth purpose in psychological science (although not as many as one might expect), and Rick Warren's 2003 blockbuster *The Purpose-Driven Life* drew widespread public attention to the concept, from a devoutly religious perspective. The new field of positive psychology also has been shining a welcome spotlight on the benefits of purpose.[5] But still, in our efforts to work constructively with the young, purpose is an underutilized tool. Despite all the talk about purpose in the mass media and in other popular settings, purpose remains a marginal concern in the human sciences, in most of our families, and in practically all of our schools—in other words, in just about all of the places that try to understand young people in order to promote their healthy development. My hope is that this book may help change that.

WD
Palo Alto, CA
January 2008

THE PATH TO PURPOSE

1

Young Lives Adrift

The life prospects of a young person in today's world are far from certain. Only a few decades ago, almost all young people knew by the end of adolescence where they would live, what their occupation would be, and whom they were going to marry. Today, most young people have no answers to these questions well into adulthood. The global economy has increased the opportunities, and pressures, for young people to move far from the communities that they grew up in. Even many of the best-educated will spend years in casual jobs without settling into a permanent line of work—and, indeed, the whole notion of a permanent line of work has come into question, as many careers are evolving into a succession of relatively short-term, disconnected jobs. As for establishing their own families, young adults all over the world are deferring or declining marriage. If current trends continue, an increasing share of the youth population will never marry, or may wait until their childbearing years are almost past.[1]

Some of today's young welcome these changes and the new opportunities they offer. These young people have formulated clear aspirations for their future. They are strongly motivated, full of energy, optimistic, and have created realistic plans to accomplish their ambitions. Confident in themselves, they enjoy exploring the world and testing the limits of their potential. Far from needing any protection or prodding, they almost can't be held back. In a word, they have found a strong sense of *purpose* to inspire them and provide them with direction.

At the same time, many of their peers are floundering. In the face of the serious choices ahead of them as they move toward adulthood, they feel as though they are drifting or stalled in their personal and social development. A large portion of today's young people are hesitating to make commitments to any of the roles that define adult life, such as parent, worker, spouse, or citizen.

This delayed commitment among the young is taking place today all over the industrial world, from the United States to Japan to Europe. In Italy, to cite one extreme case, it has been reported that the *majority* of thirty-year-olds still live at home with their parents and are neither married nor fully employed. In the United States, a study of youth in their late teens and early twenties concluded: "Marriage, home, and children are seen by most of them not as achievements to be pursued but as perils to be avoided."[2]

The British government was the first to officially recognize the growing phenomenon of unoccupied young adults when, in a national report five years ago, it coined the term "Young NEETs" ("Not in Education, Employment, or Training").[3] Recently, the Japanese government has reported, with evident alarm, that almost a million of its own youthful population had become NEETs—and this in a society long known for its strong intergenerational work ethic. None of these reports has cited any economic slowdown as the problem. The economy in Europe, Asia, the United States, and other parts of the industrial world has been growing rapidly enough to offer plentiful employment opportunities for the young. But many are holding back. Perhaps they are daunted by the uncertainties they face, perhaps they are fearful of perils they perceive in the choices they might make, or perhaps they consider the prospects available to them to be uninspiring and devoid of meaning. The reasons behind their hesitation often seem mysterious to parents and educators, many of whom are becoming concerned that these young people have yet to find the kinds of engagements and commitments that make life fulfilling.

Many parents are also voicing the concern—often humorously at first, but less so over time—that their progeny may become "boomerangers," returning to their home nests long after they were supposed to have flown away on their own wings. I've come to call this the "How can I get my wonderful daughter to move out of our basement?" question. Of course, not all parents are troubled by seeing their children take some extra time to strike out on their own, and there is a positive side to the story: it does indicate a closeness that has eluded many families in prior decades. These days, grown children feel comfortable staying in their family homes, and they do actually seem to enjoy hanging around their parents and communicating with them much more openly than did people of the boomer generation when they themselves were young.

A bit of light on this matter was shed by a May 2007 *Fortune* magazine piece on "baby boomers' kids," written delightfully by Nadira Hira, who identifies herself as one of those kids.[4] Extolling (correctly) the extraordinary talent, energy, and creativity that mark her cohort of young people, the author makes the case that "all that questioning" that her peers are doing "will lead us to some important answers." In the meantime, the extended period of questioning and self-exploration is delaying that transition to permanent work and a home of their own far beyond that of any prior generation. Hira cites a survey of American college students from 2000 through 2006 showing that almost two thirds of the graduates moved home after college and over half of these stayed for more than a year. She quotes one twenty-eight-year-old (who himself wrote a book on the subject[5]) as saying: "If we don't like a job, we quit, because the worst thing that can happen is that we move back home. There's no stigma . . . our moms would love nothing more than to cook our favorite meatloaf." Another young adult, a twenty-four-year-old woman, echoes this sentiment: "I think parents want to feel needed, and it's like, because I'm so independent, they get excited when I ask for a favor."

Now, parental love for children is one of the world's great blessings; and it is true, fortunately, that most parents will gladly do anything to help their children get along. Also, it is unambiguously a good thing that most children feel secure in their expectations that parents will provide for their needs. But I am not convinced that most parents hope to spend their golden years providing basic needs for their children; nor do I believe that this truly would be in the best interests of the children themselves. What *is* in children's best interests is to find ways to make their own contributions to their families and eventually to the world beyond themselves.

The ultimate problem is not the parent's role in the child's life but rather the child's own personal fulfillment. During the adolescent years, a certain amount of soul-searching and experimentation is healthy. Adolescence is a transitory period of development, a kind of way station on the road to a mature self-identity.[6] This formative period of life is said to begin with the onset of puberty and end with a firm commitment to adult social roles, such as those cited earlier: parent, spouse, worker, and citizen.[7] During this key time of transition to adulthood, it is sensible for young people to spend time examining themselves, considering their futures, and looking around for the opportunities that best suit their own ambitions and interests. For many young people, an extended period of exploration and reflection during adolescence may be necessary to establish a fulfilling self-identity and a positive direction in life. This is what the renowned psychologist Erik Erikson once described as a constructive "moratorium" from reality. And yes, this "identity formation" task in some cases can take years of postponing choices in order to resolve the task successfully.[8]

Yet the postponements of many young people today have taken on a troubling set of characteristics, and chief among them is that so many youth do not seem to be moving toward any resolution. Their delay is characterized more by indecision than by motivated reflection, more by confusion than by the pursuit of clear goals, more by ambivalence than by determination. Directionless drift is not a constructive moratorium in either a developmental or a societal sense. Without a sense of direction, opportunities are lost, and doubt and self-absorption can set in. Maladaptive habits are established and adaptive ones are not built. It is not that there is a critical period for the acquisition of a fruitful direction in life. But it is the case that excessive delay beyond the period of readiness creates the serious risk that the young person may give up altogether on the tasks of finding a positive direction, sustaining that direction, and acquiring the skills needed to achieve the directional goals.

Today's young people are well aware that they will need to make a transition from adolescence to adulthood at some point; but for too many of them, this awareness—which can be a source of keen anticipation for those who look to their futures with hope—triggers a sense of vague foreboding or worse, a debilitating anxiety that can lead to further developmental paralysis. Indeed, extended disengagement from adult social roles is a prescription for anxiety and depression. To remain uncommitted to career, family, and other serious community responsibilities is an untenable position for a young person to settle into. Such disengagement becomes increasingly uncomfortable over time. It cannot continue indefinitely without psychological costs.

I do not wish to suggest that most of today's young are in "deep trouble" or any kind of immediate peril. In fact, the most visible indicators of youth well-being look somewhat better today, or at least not worse, than they did ten or fifteen years ago. In the United States, today's young people are less likely than the young of ten years ago to become pregnant while still teenagers; they are less prone to violence and crime; they are somewhat less vulnerable to the lure of addictive drugs; and they are no more prone to major eating disorders (with the exception of obesity, which is still on the rise among youngsters and adults alike). Most students are staying in school for more years and are attending classes with greater regularity. Students are working harder and learning a bit more, at least judging from the most recent test-score results. Many young people fill their schedules with wholesome activities, from sports to arts to hiking and camping clubs. Although the "problems of youth" that made so many headlines in the United States a decade ago have certainly not all been solved, they have stopped going in the wrong direction, and in many areas there has been gradual and marked progress. Indeed, many young people today are thriving, as I noted at the outset.

But others only appear to be doing well, and far too many seem stuck, rudderless and lacking a sense of what they want to do with their lives. They may be keeping out of trouble and achieving what we ask of them, but actually they are drifting, without a clear sense of direction. They look like they are on track, but they may be only a step away from falling—or jumping—off the track that they appeared to be on. Many are themselves aware that something is missing from their lives, although often they can articulate their awareness only indirectly, through expressions of anxiety ("so stressed out!"), cynicism ("like I should care?"), or apathy ("Whatever!"). Few people around them know what is bothering these youngsters, except in extreme cases where a failure to thrive of crisis proportions brings the aimlessness unavoidably to light.

What is too often missing—not altogether absent but evident only in a minority of today's youth—is the kind of wholehearted dedication to an activity or interest that stems from a serious purpose, a purpose that can give meaning and direction to life.

A STUDY OF YOUTH PURPOSE

How bad is the problem really? About seven years ago, I began an investigation into what happens when a young person finds (or does not find) purpose in life. From my earlier observations of adolescents and young adults making their way through today's world, I had come to suspect that much of the difference between young people who were thriving and those who were floundering could be explained by whether or not they had found a compelling purpose—in a career, in building a family of their own, or in some other way of making a difference in the world. I also suspected that the discontent or anxiety that so many young people were feeling was connected to purpose-lessness. As I will address in more detail later, a good deal of work in psychology has revealed that there is a powerful link between the pursuit of a positive purpose and life satisfaction.

In my investigation into the role of purpose in young lives, I and my team of researchers have conducted a series of studies that has included surveys and in-depth interviews with adolescents and young adults in several parts of the United States. We have also developed case studies of some young people who have demonstrated truly extraordinary commitments to purpose, many of whom discovered such purpose at an early age. In chapters 3 and 4 of this book, I report highlights from the first of these studies.[9] For now, I will simply note that our initial findings reveal a society in which purposefulness among young people is the exception rather than the rule.

In our interviews and surveys, only about one in five young people in the 12–22-year age range express a clear vision of where they want to go, what they want to accomplish in life, and why. The largest portion of those we interviewed—almost 60 percent—may have engaged in some potentially purposeful activities, or they may have developed some vague aspirations; but they do not have any real commitment to such activities or any realistic plans for pursuing their aspirations. The remaining portion of today's youth population—almost a quarter of those we interviewed in the first of our studies—express no aspirations *at all*. In some cases, they claim that they see no point in acquiring any.

Tommy, an eighteen-year-old from Pennsylvania, is one of those who expressed absolutely no sense of purpose when we interviewed him.[10] He was halfway through his freshman year in college at the time, and had not yet been at all motivated by anything he had studied in school. Nor did he consider that there was any good reason to drop out. He knew of no better alternatives outside the university, and he had found the schoolwork easy enough. In fact, Tommy said he was quite content to just drift. He complacently conveyed a conviction that things would surely work out one way or another, whether or not he mobilized himself to do anything about it; and, since he had no particular goal in mind, he was indifferent to exactly how his future might take shape.

Tommy's indifference applied to his everyday decisions as well as his broader reflections. On the issue of choosing his academic program, he said, "I don't know what I'm going to take next term. They make you pick some courses. I'll just say 'what the hell' and flip a coin or something." On the question of aspirations, Tommy was quite comfortable with having none: "I don't really have goals for my future. What's the big deal about that? It would be fun to travel. I'd like that, especially if I could get someone to pay for it."

Tommy is one of a number of young people today who express no need for goals or ambitions. Some of these disaffected, like Tommy himself, show little sign of being bothered by their lack of direction. Another boy we interviewed, a seventeen-year-old from New Jersey, embraced his purposelessness in the following manner: "Apathy seems to have worked out well for me. . . . If you don't care, things don't bother you. So far, just being lazy and letting the chips fall where they may has been all right."

At least for the present, such young people have no complaints about their emotional states and often proclaim that they feel happy enough. But can purposelessness provide a route to happiness, in the way that they seem to assume? Certainly purposelessness can be compatible with hedonism, and many disengaged youngsters do report that they are having a good time. But, as psychologists who have studied happiness in recent years have found, the moments of hedonistic pleasure that disengaged people may experience are short-lived and ultimately empty, especially in comparison with the more enduring and fulfilling types of satisfaction that the psychologist Martin Seligman has called "authentic" happiness.[11] And many disengaged youngsters are far from happy, even in the hedonistic sense.

For many disengaged youth, the lack of direction is a good deal more troubling. They report an inner life of anxiety and a sense of feeling trapped in a life that is not under their own control. They feel disappointed in themselves and discouraged by what life has offered them thus far. They despair at the emptiness and meaninglessness of their daily activities.

Ben, age twelve, was already "worried about what I'm going to be when I grow up" when we interviewed him. He told us that he spends most of his time on his schoolwork but takes little satisfaction from it. Most of the time, he says, "I want to go outside and just relax and do nothing at all." Ben's main reason for studying so hard is pressure from his mother, who "thinks that I should just study . . . she wants me to be the best student of all her friends." In his mother's view, Ben's future lies in learning technical skills in order to qualify for a good job. Ben, on the other hand, loves music and imagines that he would like to become a singer or a dancer someday. For this aspiration, Ben gets no family support: My mom "wants me to have my own choices, but she wants my choices to be math and science." As a result, Ben feels disengaged from his day-to-day activities, which he feels have been thrust upon him by external forces. He complies dutifully but unhappily: "I like acting, singing, those things I really like, but my mom says, 'No, you shouldn't' . . . I'm locked inside a cage."

Ben has been frustrated by his inability to stake out a direction that he can call his own. He can see that the future his parents have in mind for him will not be meaningful to him, and this realization makes him feel trapped and anxious. Ben may have time to gain support for pursuing his own interests while still in his school years. For other young people, the realization that the paths they are on will not lead to a sense of purpose may take longer. Often those who have failed to find that purpose are surprised when, in their young adult years, they are blindsided by sudden feelings of emptiness and misery as they survey the directions their lives have taken.

Jessica, now twenty-seven, is a young woman who has done everything right in her schooling and early jobs.[12] She attended a prestigious independent school and college, was awarded a fellowship to a top graduate program, and received several offers from firms wanting to recruit her. She was something of a star in school and college, athletically as well as academically. Yet Jessica never considered herself to be an intellectual or a dedicated sportswoman. In fact, other than traveling for pleasure or hanging out with her friends, there have been no activities in her life that she has found consistently pleasurable. Although she did well in most of her courses, none of them ever sparked her interest to the extent that she did more than cursory reading about the subject matter in her free time. She exercises regularly because she wants to look good, but she has lost interest in the sports she played; and other than movies she rarely bothers to attend cultural events.

Jessica says that she cannot escape the feeling that "everything I've been doing my whole life has been for someone else—my parents, teachers, coaches, everyone but me. And I don't ever want to disappoint them." Worse, despite her obvious talents, she feels inauthentic. "I've been faking it all my life," she once exclaimed. She doubts whether she really knows enough to excel at a complex job; and she is even less certain that any of the occupations she can imagine for herself will hold her interest. As a consequence, she experiences panic spells when thinking about her future. At the present time, she does not feel able to follow up on any of her recent job offers. Instead, she has decided to take some time off to travel until she acquires a firmer fix on where she wants to go in life. Hers is a reasonable decision, but it is accompanied by much painful self-doubt and anxiety.

Jessica lies somewhere in the middle of the spectrum of those lacking in purpose. She is not damaged in any deep sense but also not on the verge of finding a direction that she feels enthusiastic about. Like many in her cohort, Jessica dwells uneasily in a state of drawn-out anxiety and confusion that shows no sign of ending. "I never really decided that this is what I want to be doing; it just kind of happened," she says. "I think that's the reason I want to get away all the time—I never quite feel that I'm where I want to be or should be."

Jessica is disappointed that her past achievements, applauded as they were by her parents and teachers, have not helped her identify a goal or course of action that she really desires. The outcome of her situation is far from certain. She may "find herself" during her self-imposed moratorium; or she may drift from one transient setting to another for the duration of her youth, failing to find lasting meaning in anything she does.

Some of Jessica's peers are in a good deal worse shape. They lack Jessica's record of achievement, her proven talents, and the reliable support from family and friends that Jessica can draw on as she struggles with her frustrations. And studies have shown that many of those young people are suffering from a range of psychological symptoms, stress symptoms that go beyond Jessica's sporadic feelings of panic: sleep disturbances, eating disorders, uncontrolled anger, social isolation, sexual dysfunction, substance abuse, and a host of other self-destructive tendencies.

Anthony Seldon, the Master of Wellington College in the United Kingdom, remarked in a recent newspaper column: "Depression and hyper-anxiety among the young at school and university . . . have reached epidemic proportions. A Harley Street psychiatrist last year reported that he was seeing five distressed children from just one class from a highly academic 'successful' London school. Is it surprising that at university so many find it difficult to cope? Recent U.S. studies show 45% of undergraduates display serious signs of depression. This is madness." [13]

In a recent book about today's "generation of disconnected and unhappy kids," the clinical psychologist Madeline Levine describes a pattern of inner emptiness that she has observed in the troubled teenagers she treats in her practice. Some of these youngsters exhibit seriously self-destructive behavior—for example, one fifteen-year-old girl who actually carved the word "empty" on her left forearm. "Cutting" of this sort has been brought to parents' attention through a good deal of coverage in the media, but fortunately it is still a relatively rare phenomenon. Of particular interest for us here are Levine's observations about the less troubled kids who come to see her with more typical adolescent concerns. "Many of these teens," she writes, "have a notable ability to put up a good front." Yet they complain about feelings of anxiety and emptiness: "they are certainly unhappy." They show little enthusiasm for any of their pursuits, and they have trouble finding pleasure in their daily activities. Some of the phrases that they use to describe their angst include: "being at loose ends," "unhappy for no reason," and, most tellingly, "missing something inside."[14]

Even among the highest-achieving of this group of adolescents, observers have noticed a puzzling lack of sustained commitment to the activities that have led to their early success. In a recent *New York Times* story, education writer Laura Pappano chronicled a group of top students she calls "the incredibles," mostly because they have accomplished so much in secondary school that they find college a letdown, with little challenge left to sustain their interest.[15] One MIT student responds by spending time on water polo, Frisbee, surfing, and TV.

The author's point was that expectations for students have ratcheted up to such an extent that the brightest students may be achieving too much too soon for their own long-term interests—and, what's more, such students eventually pose problems for an educational system that doesn't keep the pressure on once the student reaches the university. She quotes one higher education administrator who comments: "We are pushing kids to do so many things to get in, so what do you do when you get in?"

But I would make a different point: These brilliant students would not be losing their motivation in college *if they brought with them a better understanding of what they wanted to accomplish and why*. If, during the early years of strenuous effort and high achievement, they had found purposes that went deeper than the grades and awards, they would have hit the ground running when they entered college. They would then have been eager to gain more knowledge and skills in order to help them better accomplish their chosen purposes.

The adverse psychological effects of this aimlessness during the college years are cause for concern. The distress of apparently successful but directionless young people can boil over into self-destructive behavior when it is least expected. In our colleges and universities, legions of high-performing students attempt suicide each year.[16] Far too many succeed. In its most recent report on suicide among adolescents and young adults, the U.S. Centers for Disease Control and Prevention documented an 8 percent rise in the latest year on record (2004), the largest rise in more than fifteen years.[17] Within the halls of higher education, there has been growing concern about suicide risks among students in recent years. Almost invariably, college counselors chalk the problem up to stress caused by the heavy burdens of schoolwork and competition. I am in full sympathy with the concern over desperately unhappy students, but I am unconvinced by the "stress" explanation. Hard work and competition have never broken the spirits of young people, as long as they believe in what they are doing.

In a study that followed seven thousand American teenagers from eighth grade through high school, Barbara Schneider and David Stevenson came to a surprising conclusion: Contrary to popular (or media!) images of hedonistic, fun-crazed youth, most of today's young do have ambitions they would like to achieve. Yet few of them have any real prospect of realizing these ambitions. "Most high school students . . . ," the authors write, "have high ambitions but no clear life plans for reaching them." They are, in the authors' phrase, "motivated but directionless." As a consequence, they become increasingly frustrated, depressed, and alienated. There seems to be some hidden anguish in the misery of the youths that Schneider and Stevenson describe. What's more, the hidden nature of this misery is part of the problem itself; as they observe, many parents seem unaware of the problem, and as I will address more fully later, the authors also point out that "many parents do not see it as their responsibility to actively help their adolescents form plans for their futures."[18]

A 2005 PBS documentary, *Declining by Degrees*, documents the disillusionment and disengagement pervasive among university students today.[19] The documentary shows students sleeping through classes, shirking their assignments, partying several nights of the week, and in many cases drinking their way through their four-year college "education." The film was meant as a stinging critique of higher education, but the view that it provides of student attitudes is at least as revealing as its view of our university system. The students portrayed are bright and friendly, often with reasonably good academic records (even those who rarely open a book seem to get passing grades or better). From a distance, considering the terrible conditions that people find themselves in around the world, it may be hard to see what these privileged youth find lacking in their lives. Yet something certainly is missing. In the past, some educators have called this missing element "motivation," and I agree that sufficient motivation is indeed lacking. But I would also argue that the core problem is the lack of a *source* of motivation, the lack of a sense of purpose. In the long run, that lack of purpose can destroy the foundations of a happy and fulfilled life.

UNCOMMITTED AND YET TO EMERGE

Of course, every generation has had young people who have resisted the conventions of adulthood. In a prescient book called *The Uncommitted: Alienated Youth in American Society* (1965), Kenneth Keniston wrote of a group of young college men who, despite their privileged status (they were all Harvard students), had become deeply disaffected from our society. These so-called alienated students expressed cynicism about virtually all mainstream values, social roles, and institutions that they had encountered in the world around them. Although well educated and highly articulate, they had no larger beliefs or life plans. Their alienation, Keniston wrote, was ideological in character: these students had made a conscious, intellectually driven choice to remain uncommitted.

Although *The Uncommitted* attracted intense interest when it appeared, the young people the book profiled were, as Keniston wrote, "not typical of American youth."[20] They were but a sliver of the population. Even among their sophisticated classmates, they stood out as extreme in their intellectualized skepticism about society's misdirections.[21] Few of their peers shared their malaise. Although these "uncommitted" students were fascinating to behold (perhaps because they may have seemed like harbingers of things to come), their significance to the broader American society of the time was never clear.

The lack of commitment among the young today is of quite a different sort than that which Keniston described. It has none of the sharp ideological edges that the alienated youth of midcentury America expressed. Today's noncommitment has no personal, social, or political point; it has no focus or objective. In an unintended way, this makes it a purer form of noncommitment, a noncommitment even to noncommitment. It is neither a dedication *toward* something nor a reaction *against* something. It is, rather, an absence of something—a kind of empty space in a panorama that, in other times and places, has been filled with dynamic activity.

Other researchers have identified this trend but have viewed it more sanguinely than I do, or have put forth different explanations for it. For example, the psychologist Jeffrey Arnett begins his book *Emerging Adulthood* with an astute observation: "In the past few decades a quiet revolution has taken place for young people in American society, so quiet that it has been noticed only gradually and incompletely." Arnett goes on to argue that in light of the way adolescence has extended so much, we need to designate a new life stage, which he dubs "emerging adulthood": this is the "quiet revolution" that he alludes to.

Arnett's take on the phenomenon is largely optimistic, with no more than a hint of ambivalence: "To be a young American today is to experience both excitement and uncertainty, wide-open possibility and confusion, new freedoms and new fears."[22] In Arnett's view, the upside of today's lengthy period of "emergence" is that it provides young adults with an optimal chance to work out a well-planned future, tailored to their own special talents, interests, and desires. But I would argue that this optimism is appropriate for only a minor portion of the youth population. For the rest, increased attention on our part is a more appropriate response.

I also do not think that we are in general pushing youngsters too hard, as some have argued. Madeline Levine puts the blame for the aimlessness of young people on too-high expectations, parental pressure, and family affluence. My own view is that young people thrive on high expectations (I wrote a book on this matter ten years ago),[23] and that parents do well to engage attentively with their children. As for affluence, our research has found similar patterns among groups of affluent and nonaffluent youngsters: A small portion of young people in both the affluent and nonaffluent groups are strongly directed and deeply engaged; most in both groups are searching for something positive to give their lives meaning; and a significant minority in each group show little sign of trying to find something worthwhile. So I believe that we must look further than these explanations.

This is where the role of purpose comes in, and we must be concerned because the demoralizing effects of failing to discover a clear and authentic sense of purpose in life can last a long time, even a lifetime.

UNFULFILLED IN MIDLIFE

A few years ago, I met with a group of students who had just started a teacher education program. The group included some recent college graduates. But there were also a number of more mature people as well, students in their thirties or forties. What had brought them here, after what must have been years of doing something else? Why, I wondered, had they taken this new direction in their lives?

After the meeting I spoke with the students and discovered that the older students had dropped out of law, medicine, the military, and business. They had not failed in the eyes of the world. Some had found good jobs in the corporate or professional world. Yet they all had quit, with pretty much the same complaint: they never acquired a sense that they were doing something that really mattered to them.

They felt empty and inauthentic. They shared a depressing sense that they were wasting their time on activities that did not reflect their own highest aspirations in life. In short, they felt burned out at an early age. Whatever they had begun had not sustained their enthusiasm for even a small part of their early adulthood, let alone for much of their working lives.

At least the students with whom I spoke had moved on in midlife to identify an interest that might give them a shot at a meaningful pursuit. Perhaps they will find what they are looking for in a teaching career, or perhaps not—only time will tell. In other cases that I have encountered, early failures to find personally meaningful work have simmered in a stew of anxious frustration and confusion, leading nowhere. Often it is the people who seem to be most on track who express the most severe misgivings. A thirty-year-old cardiologist recently asked me for advice. In his brief career, this brilliant young man already had acquired a reputation as one of the southeastern United States's top experts in complex surgical heart procedures. Naturally, his services were much in demand. The problem was that he hated his work to such a degree that he could barely get out of bed in the morning. Although he tried to take satisfaction in the life-saving work that he did for his patients, he could not escape the feeling that from early childhood he had always managed his life to please other people. His unhappiness was evident in the restless manner in which he sat and spoke about his dread of a future that might feel to him like the present. When I talked with him, he was on the verge of walking away from his long medical training to search for a job he could find more personally meaningful. He did not have the vaguest idea what that job would be. Yet his discomfort was so great that leaping into the unknown seemed to him a better alternative than staying on his present path.

Contrast this story with one from the PBS documentary I mentioned earlier. Not every student in *Declining by Degrees* ended up drifting through college or dropping out. One of those who stuck with it was a young woman named Brittany. Like many of the other students the film portrayed, Brittany became discouraged because, she said, "I didn't have anything that kept me wanting to come to campus. I wasn't being challenged, I wasn't really thinking about things . . . I was just, like, 'I have no idea who I am, what I'm going to do, what I want to do,' it was really alarming." But Brittany got lucky, unlike most students in the documentary. Right before she was about to leave the college, she stumbled into a course in planetary physics, which she took to meet her science requirement. Unexpectedly, she got interested in the subject matter. The instructor noticed her interest (mainly because this interest alone was unusual enough to make her stand out from her peers), and he sat her down for a serious talk. The conversation persuaded Brittany that she might have an aptitude for science, that she might even have a calling for it. When Brittany finished college, she enrolled in a graduate program in planetary physics. "Sometimes," the instructor later mused, "just a little bit of encouragement makes all the difference."

But if this is so, why are so many of the other students left to flounder? Where is the guidance—the "little bit of encouragement"—that today's young may need to find a sense of purpose?

I argue in this book that a significant part of the problem is that the phenomenon of purposelessness is not widely enough recognized by those to whom young people look for guidance. Indeed, it is not even on the radar screens of the agents of culture that influence young people—mass media, schools, or civic and religious organizations. Although there is a great deal of care and concern for young people throughout our society, there is not a great deal of understanding about this issue; it is time to focus on how we can help them to discover the life purposes they are searching for.

PURPOSE, COMMITMENT, AND THE WELL-BEING OF YOUTH AND SOCIETY

Why does a sense of purpose matter? What does it do for young people to approach their futures with a sense of inspiration and noble aspiration? Of course, the benefits for society are not hard to see. Without a younger generation dedicated to taking up the challenges of a world that needs a lot of repairing, it is hard to imagine how a decent future can be achieved. But my primary concern in this book is not with society; it is with young people themselves. The case that I make throughout this book is that finding a clear purpose in life is essential for their achievement of happiness and satisfaction in life, and that doing so is a good deal harder than it should be in our present-day cultural environment.

What exactly do I mean by a "life purpose"? A purpose is an *ultimate concern*. It is the final answer to the question *Why? Why* are you doing this? *Why* does it matter to you? *Why* is it important? A purpose is a deeper reason for the immediate goals and motives that drive most daily behavior.

Short-term desires come and go. A young person may desire a good grade on a test, a date to the prom, a cutting edge electronic

PlayStation, a starting slot on the basketball team, or admission to a prestigious college. These are desires; they reflect immediate aims that may or may not have longer-term significance. A purpose, by contrast, is an end in itself.

A person can change purposes, or add new ones, over the years; but it is in the nature of purposes to endure at least long enough that a serious commitment is made and some progress toward that aim is achieved. A purpose can organize an entire life, imparting not only meaning but also inspiration and motivation for ongoing learning and achievement.

How do we help young people find a path to purpose? The good news is that we now know enough about the value of purpose in a young person's life, as well as about how young people can develop a sense of purpose, that we can take some active steps to help steer youngsters effectively onto the path. In the next chapter, I will introduce important findings from developmental psychology and the newer field of positive psychology about how and why a sense of purpose plays such a valuable role in our lives. Chapters 3 and 4 describe results from our own studies of youth purpose. In the concluding chapters I offer some recommendations for how those who wish to help young people find positive purposes can play a constructive—perhaps decisive—role in getting them on their way.

2

Why Purpose Is Crucial for Thriving Throughout Life

"A person without purpose is like a ship without a rudder," wrote the Scottish historian and philosopher Thomas Carlyle almost two hundred years ago. More recently, religious, scientific, and popular writings have drawn attention to the importance of purpose in human life. Church leader Rick Warren's book *The Purpose-Driven Life*, for example, gained a large popular audience for his religious view that the central task on earth is finding God's purpose for us.[1] Warren's treatment of purpose springs from his Christian faith; but his book has had broad influence beyond religious readers, and it includes many insights into the personal benefits of purpose as well. Warren convincingly argues that purpose adds both energy and resilience to our lives. Increased energy springs from the feelings of inspiration that a belief in the purpose provides, while increased resilience springs from the steady dedication to something larger than ourselves. This steady dedication counteracts our destructive tendencies toward self-absorption.

In the past few years, the brain and behavioral sciences, and even medical research, have also begun paying considerable attention to purpose and related concepts such as "meaning," "intentional goals," and "ultimate concerns," and the roles they play in well-being. Study after study has found a person's sense of life purpose to be closely connected to virtually all dimensions of well-being. Recent studies in neuroscience, for example, have found that certain areas of the brain show a strong response when people observe or engage in intentional activities. Particular neuronal webs, located in sections of the brain that govern social and moral judgments, fire when actions are seen as purpose-driven.[2] Studies of aging have shown that one of the prime predictors of health and well-being in old age is whether a person continues to be purposeful.[3] Researchers studying people with mental health problems and disabilities have found that helping them find a sense of purpose can assist them in overcoming their psychological deficits.[4] The implication of these studies is that a disposition toward purposeful activity has been bred into us and plays a central role in energizing and guiding many of us through the most important choices that we make in life.

In psychology, there is a rich tradition of studies in purpose and meaning, and a strong empirical case has been built for Carlyle's claim that purpose functions like a rudder that keeps us mentally on course. Interestingly, that case has been made from a number of quite distinct, and even opposing, viewpoints.

The field of clinical psychology, and its understanding of the role of purpose, was profoundly influenced by the publication in 1946 of a landmark book by a psychologist and Holocaust survivor: Viktor Frankl's *Man's Search for Meaning*. The Nazis murdered Frankl's wife, parents, and grandparents, and Frankl himself suffered through three years of concentration camp internment. As a camp inmate, he was subjected to slave labor, torture, starvation rations, and other horribly harsh conditions. He found that it was only his determination to make sense out of his hardships—and to write about his reflections in a way that would be edifying for others—that enabled him to survive.

Frankl clung to the manuscript that he wrote like a life raft, and later published it to great acclaim. He observed that those inmates who held purposeful belief systems, such as religious faith or conviction about human progress, were far more likely to survive the camp's hardships than those who simply tried to eke out their existence. He went on to create an approach to clinical psychology, called "Logotherapy," based on the insight that purpose and meaning promote mental health by serving as protective factors against depression and a host of anxiety disorders. This was a radical idea at the time, because most clinicians were imbued with the Freudian view that neuroses were subconscious, requiring in-depth analysis to treat. Frankl was one of the early pioneers of a "cognitive revolution" in psychology, which took seriously the power of the reasoning mind to establish mental health by building positive belief systems based on purpose and meaning.

Erik Erikson, writing from the viewpoint of psychoanalytic theory, identified "purposefulness" as a key criterion of "vital individual strength" during our adult years. He argued that an essential task of our earlier years is to emerge from childhood with "a realistic sense of ambition and purpose."[5] From another perspective, the social psychologist Carol Ryff and her colleagues have reported strong associations among purpose, personal growth, relationship-building skills, a sense of command over one's life, and a positive self-image. These elements, Ryff believes, are the central components of well-being, essential for both health and happiness.[6]

The emerging discipline of positive psychology, which studies the key motivators of human happiness, and is often referred to as "happiness studies," has shown that a sense of purpose is prominent among the list of character traits that lead to happiness.[7] Foundational in this new area of science were a set of findings that combined the insights of psychology and economics and uncovered a number of counterintuitive truths about happiness. One of these findings is the intriguing paradox that the happiest people are rarely those who expend a lot of effort trying to attain pleasure for themselves.[8] In fact, many of the things that people tend to lust after in the effort to become happy seem to have little to do with it. Affluence, for example, is only marginally related to happiness—except in the case of real poverty, where more income allows for more food, better shelter, and health care. Neither do status, glory, and other attempts at ego-boosting reliably make people significantly happier: the improvements in mood that these prizes create usually prove temporary, wearing off soon after the initial glow.

What *does* matter for happiness is engaging in something that the person finds absorbing, challenging, and compelling, especially when it makes a valued contribution to the world beyond the self.[9] Scientists dedicated to discovering natural truths, artists dedicated to creating new forms of beauty, are often happiest when they are in the midst of solving a wrenchingly difficult problem.

The pursuit of noble purpose is another prime example of such engagement. A noble purpose drives a person to make a positive difference in the world. The psychologist Dan McAdams has studied adults whom he calls *generative* people, who try to make a positive difference in the world.[10] Generative adults are highly dedicated to their work and their parenting or mentoring of the young. They desire to leave a legacy behind, and they are concerned with the well-being of future generations. These people are, in other words, highly purposeful. McAdams's research has shown that generative adults are healthier and more content than other adults. They are more likely to be involved in civic activities and are more connected to families, churches, and political groups. They view the world through an optimistic lens and see themselves as highly effective. They tend to consider failure a learning opportunity, rather than allowing it to weigh them down, and they are confident that good outcomes can follow from temporary setbacks. This kind of healthy outlook on life not only produces a sense of well-being but also sets the conditions for personal success. Indeed, one substantial study of people who were celebrated for their outstanding achievements confirmed that they differed from the general population mainly in the highly developed sense of meaning that they applied to their engagements.

Recently, I and two of my students reviewed the scientific literature from developmental psychology on purpose-related phenomena and found a number of studies that demonstrate a key role for purpose in human thriving during youth and beyond.[11] Particularly interesting for parents is recent work on the role of purpose in the lives of children. In an extensive program of research, the psychologist Bonnie Benard has shown that some children can bounce back from the most severe traumas and adversities.[12] Children who respond resiliently to difficult circumstances have four key characteristics, according to Benard: a sense of purpose (extended beyond the present to a future purpose); autonomy; social competence; and problem-solving skills. Of these four, I would designate sense of purpose as the most central, because it creates the motivation for the child to establish all the others. Benard's work has been highly influential in the contemporary youth development field, and her findings on the role of purpose in childhood resilience have been replicated many times.[13]

Additional research has shown that purpose helps young people control their inner lives—including the self-destructive impulses that pop up in every young person's brain from time to time. Neuropsychological research has confirmed what everyone who spends time with young people knows: youth is a time of "ignited passions" (to borrow a phrase from the prominent brain researcher Ronald Dahl).[14] A sudden spurt in neuronal capacity around the time of puberty supercharges adolescent cognitive and emotional systems. The result is an infusion of energy into whatever captures the young person's attention. This contributes to extreme and sometimes dangerous behavior. For this reason, the period of adolescence can be hazardous to self and others. Rates of morbidity and mortality rise 200 percent during adolescence. Drunk driving is the third highest cause of teenage death, with other foolish accidents also high on the list—all of which are tragic and meaningless consequences of the brain-spurt-driven, misdirected passions of adolescence.

Yet the very same neuronal growth that creates these hard-to-control emotions and reckless behavior can improve an adolescent's judgment and reasoning capacities. The brain growth of early adolescence can expand the range of interests that young people entertain, and it can improve the degree of seriousness with which a youngster takes up these interests. Teenagers can—and do—become just as passionate about playing musical instruments or writing computer software, for example, as about driving cars too fast when drunk. The question is: Which choice will the young person make?

As Ronald Dahl notes:

> So these igniting passions can be aligned in healthy ways—in the service of higher-order goals. Feelings of passion are rooted in the same deep brain systems as biologic drives and the primitive elements of emotion. Yet passion intertwines with the highest level of human endeavor: passion for ideas and ideals, passion for beauty, passion for music and art. And the passion to succeed in a sport, business, or politics, and passion towards a person, activity, object, or pursuit can also inspire transcendent feelings.[15]

In subsequent chapters of this book—and especially in chapter 4—we shall see how purposeful young people turn their passions to productive pursuits in precisely the way that Dahl suggests.

Purpose endows a person with joy in good times and resilience in hard times, and this holds true all throughout life. Adolescence and emerging adulthood are particularly affected, however, by the presence of purpose, and purposeful youth (as we shall see) not only avoid the risks of self-destructive behavior but also show a markedly positive attitude that triggers an eagerness to learn about the world.

Purpose leads to personal satisfaction by bringing people outside themselves and into an engrossing set of activities. People with purpose stop thinking about themselves, becoming fascinated instead by the work or problem at hand. As they muster their mental and physical capacities to reach a solution, they may discover powers that they never thought they had: untried talents, new skills, reservoirs of untapped energy. They feel a surge of excitement as they move toward their objective. They lose track of everyday cares and woes, of where they happen to be, of what time it is—in short, of all the mental boundaries usually posed by our physical and material worlds. In such cases, they experience that sublime state of inspiration that the psychologist Mihaly Csikszentmihalyi has termed "flow."[16] The research is clear: while absorption in purposeful tasks may be strenuous, it also brings a deep sense of satisfaction, well-being, and exhilaration.

The paradox is that the exertion of hard and often thankless effort in service of a purpose, with little thought of personal gain, is a surer path to happiness than the eager pursuit of happiness for its own sake. Self-absorption and self-indulgence simply do not work as successful strategies for achieving happiness. People end up feeling empty and resentful because they have failed to satisfy one of our species' truest and deepest desires: the universal yearning for a life with meaning. What's more, self-absorption is emotionally destabilizing. A dedicated pursuit of purpose creates an emotional steadiness, a life that combines forward movement with stability. Virtually everyone who has written about psychological contentment has identified this combination of a sense of positive, forward direction and emotional stability as one of its key conditions.

THE SURE SIGNS OF PURPOSE

But what exactly *is* purpose? And how can we know it when we see it?

Any word can be used in multiple ways, but for the sake of careful analysis it is necessary to select one precise definition and stick with it.

Someone can always quibble about whether the definition includes every nuance the word may suggest, but a definition at least makes fundamentally clear what we are talking about. In the review of the scientific literature that I noted above, we found a rough consensus in the way that research in human development has defined purpose over the years.[17] We honed and cleaned up the language and came up with the following definition:

Purpose is a stable and generalized intention to accomplish something that is at the same time meaningful to the self and consequential for the world beyond the self.

We chose this definition because it highlights two key points: (1) Purpose is a goal of sorts, but it is more far-reaching and more stable than common lower-level goals such as "to have a good time tonight," "to find a parking place in town," "to buy an inexpensive pair of shoes that look nice," or "to pass that chemistry test." (2) Purpose may play a part in one's personal search for meaning, but it goes beyond personal meaning and therefore is not strictly synonymous with it. Purpose reaches out to the world beyond the self. It implies a desire to make a difference in the world, perhaps to contribute something to others, or create something new, or accomplish something of one's own. The aimed-for accomplishment can be material or nonmaterial, external or internal, realistic or purely idealistic. In many cases, a purpose may not be achievable in one's lifetime—for example, abolishing poverty or creating world peace. But an extremely ambitious goal is not necessarily naive; for many it is a practical source of intense motivation.

A true purpose is an *ultimate concern*. It is the final answer to the question of *Why? Why* am I doing this? *Why* does it matter? *Why* is it important for me and for the world beyond me? *Why* do I strive to accomplish this end? A purpose is the reason *behind* the immediate goals and motives that drive most of our daily behavior.

Goals and motives come and go. A young person may want a new car, a trip to Mexico, a good grade on a test, admission to a particular college. These are immediate goals, not ultimate concerns; they are means to more important ends. A purpose is an end *in itself*, an *ultimate* concern that drives the shorter-term goals, as in: *"I want to get good grades and go to medical school so that I can become a doctor and take care of the sick,"* or: *"I want to earn money so that I can become an entrepreneur and build a great business."* It is important to note, though, that short-term goals and a longer-term, larger purpose are not unrelated. Studies have shown that where no larger purpose exists, short-term goals and motives usually lead nowhere and soon extinguish themselves in directionless activity.[18]

Purposes can be complex and ambitious—"I want to help the nations of Africa find ways to stop the spread of malaria"—or they can be modest and familiar—"I want to have a nice family and take care of my children." They can change over time, and a person may add new ones over the years. But it is in the nature of a purpose to endure at least long enough for the person to express commitment to it in action, and usually to make some progress toward accomplishing it. The pursuit of a purpose can organize an entire life, imparting not only meaning and exhilaration but also motivation for learning and achievement.

I must note one more essential insight about purpose and its role in thriving that I learned from my studies in human development. In this case, my learning took place many years ago, at the hands of a great master of developmental theory. It stays with me to this day and still shapes my understanding of what really matters in youth development.

MY OWN EARLY EDUCATION
IN HUMAN THRIVING

When I was beginning my academic career as an assistant professor, out of the blue a kindly dean offered me a traveling fellowship to spend a month visiting Jean Piaget's lab in Geneva, Switzerland. Piaget was the most famous living developmental psychologist at the time, and his writings were a strong influence on my own early work. I was thrilled at the chance to meet the grand master, and it turned out to be just in time, as Piaget passed away the following year.

Yet in preparing for the visit, I had two significant handicaps. First, my French was abysmal, and I had only a couple of months to cram in some practice. Second, although I had devoured many of Piaget's writings with great appreciation, I (like many others in the field) had found his most recent book to be virtually undecipherable. To add to my anxiousness, this was the book in which Piaget laid out his solution to the most important and difficult mystery of all: what *causes* human development. Piaget called his answer to this question "equilibration" (also the title of the book); but, to be perfectly frank, that was almost all that I took away from it after many hours spent trying to understand the turgid text.

Nevertheless, I was determined to get everything possible out of the trip, learning firsthand the master's own solution to development's deepest mystery. When I first got to Geneva, it looked like I was in luck, because Piaget was teaching a seminar on this very topic. Clearly it was something that was at the forefront of his mind during his final days. *Le Patron* (this was what all his students and assistants called him, something I have yet to pull off in my own lab) invited me to sit in on the seminar during my month-long stay. What an opportunity! Yet soon it became apparent that Piaget's statements in the seminar were just as impenetrable as those in his book. And it was not just my shaky French: the native students told me over coffees and beers that they were every bit as lost as I was.

Finally, on the last day of my visit (the timing of which made me wonder if this was somehow meant to be), the great man said something that I actually understood and still find illuminating to this very day. He had become exasperated at one student's confusion (shared by us all, of course) over just what equilibration is and how it works in development. (Literally, the term means "achieving balance," and none of us could grasp how this creates developmental change.) Piaget asked the student: "If you fall in the water, what's the best way to stay up?" Feeling very much on the spot, the student ventured, in quick succession: "Float? Tread water? Kick your feet around a lot and keep your head up?" "NO!" Piaget thundered. "You must *swim*, and in a *direction*. You must *move forward*. That will keep you steady. Plus, you may also have the advantage of getting somewhere. *That* is what equilibration in development is. It is moving forward, steadily, never trying to stay in one place."

In the long run, Piaget's swimming metaphor has enabled me to tackle a key question that parents and educators have about guiding young people: How, exactly, can we tell when a young person is thriving, or, in other words, "on track" developmentally? What, exactly, counts as *thriving* in youth development? How can we know, before it becomes obvious due to behavioral problems, that we should be concerned?

The main problem is that any presumed behavioral indicator of thriving—or of failure to do so—can be misleading. A young person may be engaged in all sorts of activities and excelling at them, but still be lacking true direction. Or, she may seem to be up against mental or physical odds that seem insurmountable and yet be in the very process of surmounting them. For example, a pediatrician might venture that a seven-year-old child who still struggles with simple speech is not thriving and therefore suggest that this be taken as an indicator. But then there is the case of Helen Keller, a beacon of thriving during her entire life, despite the severe handicaps that retarded her speech for all of her youth. Also, it is astonishing how many Olympic athletes spent their early years fighting physical impairments; how many successful people in business had some form of learning disability; how many brilliant scientists failed elementary math; and how many world leaders struggled with social problems in their youth. How could we have determined early on that these folks were headed for success despite their apparent incapacities—that, in a developmental sense, they indeed were thriving when they were young?

Here I believe that Piaget's solution is key. More revealing than any particular behavioral signposts, such as tests passed, prizes won, or popularity gained, or even the general degree of happiness displayed, is the *direction* and *meaning* of a young person's efforts. The relevant indicators are: Is the young person attempting to move forward toward a worthwhile goal? Has the young person found fulfilling purposes to motivate and direct his or her efforts? Are the young person's purposes understood and valued by the community of people that that person needs for support while growing up?

When two crucial conditions apply: (1) *forward movement toward a fulfilling purpose*; and (2) *a structure of social support consistent with that effort*, there is every likelihood that the child will thrive. Although the young person may be struggling or even failing in some regards, in a developmental sense he or she is on track. Of course, the child must be observed over time in order to make this determination. A photo of a frustrated batter whiffing on three fastballs is not going to tell you whether he is going to hit the ball out of the park the next time at bat; nor will it tell you whether his team is going to win the game. But knowing about how the batter and his team cope with setbacks, about their determination, morale, and grit when they find themselves in tough situations, and about their *momentum* during this point in their season, will tell you a lot about whether the team is likely to prevail in the long run. Life, much like so many athletic events, is largely a game of recovery.

One of the most intriguing ideas in the developmental sciences over the past decades is the phenomenon of the "J-shaped curve." [19] While observing children learning to master new skills in dozens of domains (math, writing, the arts), psychologists noticed a surprising pattern: as a learner struggles to master difficult new challenges, there is often an initial *decline* in skill. Errors are made on tasks that previously seemed easy, and the learner feels more "stupid" than ever before. This is the dip that forms the middle part of the "J." But it turns out that the "stupid mistakes," in retrospect, were nothing more than growth errors. Once the learner gets past the dip, performance rises rapidly to new heights.

This is not merely an academic point. The subjects of our studies—young people in the midst of the bewildering, often terrifying, and always wondrous process of adolescent development—have benefited greatly when those around them were able to see that they were thriving even amid the turmoil of youth. It is when adults are able to perceive this that young people realize that there are people who believe in them. And this message can make a world of difference in the search for direction.

NOBLE AND IGNOBLE PURPOSE

One last point I should make about how to know a true sense of purpose when we see it concerns a set of tricky questions I'm often asked when I lecture: What about bad or evil purposes? Are they "true purposes" in the same sense as positive or pro-social ones? Do they work in the same way as motivators? Indeed, can we determine whether a person's purpose is good or evil, noble or ignoble?

There is no question that great evil has been done by people who commit themselves to ignoble purposes—or, perhaps more commonly, who commit ignoble deeds in the name of noble purposes. Tyrants throughout history have slaughtered people unjustly for the sake of supposed higher principles. To qualify as a worthy purpose, the *how* of a course of action, as well as its *why*, must be guided by a strong moral sense. Finding noble purpose means both devoting oneself to something worth doing *and* doing it in an honorable manner. For this reason, a telling way to distinguish between ignoble and noble purposes is to analyze whether both the means and the ends are honorable. To use an extreme example, it obviously wouldn't be noble to pursue the eradication of world poverty by exterminating people who are poor.

From my observations of purpose in human life, my readings and discussions with other scholars interested in such issues,[20] and my own reflections on the matter, I conclude that

1. Only a positive, pro-social purpose can provide the lasting inspiration, motivation, and resilience that is characteristic of a truly purposeful life. The primary reason for this is hard-wired into the natural constitution of our species: We are programmed to experience a sense of "moral elevation" when we behave benevolently and empathically toward others.[21]

2. Evil, or "ignoble," purposes may have strongly motivating effects for a period of time, but they eventually burn out, either slowly in growing doubt and uncertainty, or suddenly in self-destructive activity. Again, our biology is (in part) our destiny: We are programmed to experience "moral disgust"—not immediately and not with regularity, but eventually and unavoidably—when we behave inhumanely and act in a manner inconsistent with our core moral standards.[22]

3. Noble purposes promote the well-being of others; they are pursued through means that conform to moral standards such as honesty and respect; and they are accomplished in a spirit of reasonable humility rather than self-aggrandizement. Ignoble purposes harm others; are pursued through deceit and disrespect; and reflect egomaniacal or megalomaniacal motives. The crazed tyrant who goes to war for the supposed sake of "his people," relying on treachery, lies, and fear to maintain his power, is not hard to distinguish from the popular leader who serves by speaking the truth, listening to people's feedback, and choosing a course of action responsive to their needs.[23]

SO WHERE CAN PURPOSE BE FOUND?

In our society, work is one of the main places where people find purpose; and in work, as in every other area of life, purpose adds energy, resilience, and long-term fulfillment. In a study of Americans at midlife, psychologist Anne Colby found that workers from across the entire white/blue/pink-collar spectrum had found a sense of purpose in their jobs, seeing their work as a way to contribute to society and take responsibility for their families.[24] Bus drivers, nurses, clerks, and waitresses were just as likely to find meaning in their work as people in "elite" professions such as law and medicine. This may seem surprising in the midst of widely voiced complaints about pointless jobs replete with drudgery, corporate politics, bureaucratic paper-shuffling, and idiotic bosses. Yet this study of a nationally representative sample of Americans found that "the great majority of study participants (79%) said that their work is meaningful."[25]

There were some in just about every occupation who did not see their work as meaningful, and those people, not surprisingly, saw their jobs as little more than a burden. Yet they were in the minority, little more than 20 percent of the sample. People who are purposeful in their jobs are more likely to avoid burnout and stay committed. Young people who approach their careers with a sense of purpose resist the traps of aimless drift.

Among the sources of purpose mentioned by workers in this study were "doing a good job," "contributing to society," "helping others," "providing for my family," "supporting my fellow workers," "making a difference to the organization," "passing the work ethic down to my own children," "personal growth," and "self-expression." Interestingly, over 40 percent of the workers in the study reported that one of their satisfactions was that they had "fun" pursuing those purposes.

Traditionally, purposeful work has been known as a "calling," though the word has such a high-sounding ring to it that few people use it to refer to their own jobs (although, as I shall show, in practice most adult Americans actually do relate to their jobs as something close to callings). One unfortunate result of this is that young people rarely are encouraged to identify a calling for themselves. Rather, in a misguided attempt to be realistic, we often counsel young people to seek a vocation that will merely secure them a living, leaving the ideal of a calling as a figment of romantic fantasy. One of the ironies of this degraded view is that, linguistically at least, the term "vocation" at its root means the same thing as the word "calling": "vocation" originally comes from the Latin *vocatio*, or "to be called."

The belief in work as a calling sprang originally from ancient theological doctrine; but like many value-driven notions with religious origins, it is an idea that modern social theorists have found appealing in secular ways as well. The sociologist Max Weber wrote that all people have their own particular callings, reflecting three qualities in themselves and the world: their own abilities; the world's need for the services that their abilities can provide; and their enjoyment in serving society in their own ways.

When someone thinks of work as a calling rather than merely as a job, the experience of working is transformed. The most routine accomplishments become sources of pride. Chores that once felt like drudgery become valued ways to make a difference in other people's lives. Feelings of frustration diminish. As research has shown, these effects are true for workers in both white-collar and blue-collar jobs, in the private and public sectors, and in companies large and small.

They apply to people at the beginning of their careers, to people in their working primes, and to those who are winding down toward retirement.[26] And it is contagious: workers who feel a sense of calling inspire others to find a deeper meaning in their own work.

Vital in appreciating the role of a sense of calling is that people understand that this can be found in even what may appear to be mundane jobs and endeavors. Some years ago, I was invited to visit a small town that was concerned about the way many of its young people had been spending their time. Nothing dramatic had happened there—no tragic deaths or Columbine-type scares—but the town had been plagued with a rash of teenage drinking and driving incidents, school failures, and other standard adolescent problems. One parent told me that her son and a few of his friends had markedly improved their behavior after taking jobs at a local restaurant. Intrigued, I went by to speak with the manager. The place was a fast-food shop, serving distinctly nongourmet fare quickly to masses of customers. Still, the manager couldn't have been prouder of his operation if it were a Michelin five-star palace. "We give folks the food they enjoy at a price they can afford and make it possible for them to get on with their lives without aggravation or delay," he told me. "Families come here and go away in a better mood. Kids have fun, and Mom and Dad don't have to cook or take out a mortgage on their home to pay the check."

What about his young employees? "They always start here with an attitude. They think the customers are creeps and their job is to give them the minimum they can get away with and then head out to the rear for a smoke. I tell them that every customer must be just as important to you as your closest friend. Your job is not just to get them food and take their money. Your job is to put a smile on the customer's face. When a kid gets that, it changes everything—the attitude, the way they act, the way they dress, everything. They get a kick out of what they're doing, just like I do."

The manager's joy in his work speaks for itself. From what I could gather from my visit, the kids who worked in his fast-food joint were also enjoying their jobs, and they were not the troublesome teens whom the townsfolk were concerned about. And tellingly, they were on track in ways that extended well beyond their commitments to their jobs. The lesson in positive attitude they had learned had strengthened their motivation at school, improved their behavior in the community, and heightened their sense of themselves. They had learned that they were capable of making a tangible difference in the world, small-scale as their efforts may have seemed to others.

A purpose can be noble without being "heroic" or requiring daring, life-endangering adventures. Noble purpose *may* mean this, and our history books are full of dramatic accounts of courageous acts that really did save the day. *But noble purposes also may be found in the day-to-day fabric of ordinary existence.* A mother caring for her child, a teacher instructing students, a doctor treating patients, a citizen campaigning for a candidate for the sake of improving the community, all are pursuing noble purposes. So too are the legions of ordinary people who dedicate time, care, effort, and worldly goods to charity, to their friends and family, to their communities, to their faith, or to their responsibilities at work.

SCIENCE AND FAITH AGREE

Another powerful long-standing source for finding purpose in life is religious belief. During much of the modern era, advocates of science and advocates of faith have waged verbal battles against one another. But human purpose is one phenomenon where there are no such battles, because the traditions of science and faith say essentially the same thing. The annals of the world's great religions are full of stories about men and women who maintain their dedication and mental balance despite severe persecution and other hardships. Every religious tradition advances the notion that the closer we come to God's purpose for us, the more satisfied we shall become in our daily lives. This, as I noted earlier, is the theme of Rick Warren's influential book *The Purpose-Driven Life*. In a study of "moral exemplars" (persons who have shown extraordinary commitment to moral ideals such as compassion or justice during long periods of their lives) that Anne Colby and I completed a few years ago, we interviewed people with strong commitment to their faith. They told us that, far from feeling sorry for themselves, they felt gratitude, and even joy, for the hardships that had tested their faith. Their ordeals, they were convinced, had brought them closer to God. These people shone with purpose, and they set glowing examples for those who knew them or heard about how they had devoted their lives to feeding the hungry, fighting for civil rights, or some other noble and humane endeavor.[27]

Most of the examples in this book are drawn from secular domains such as work, family, and citizenship. But there is no question that religious purpose can promote the same kinds of positive psychological and societal benefits. In the chapters that follow I cite several examples of young people who are finding life-fulfilling purpose through faith. Yet even this age-old method has been slipping away in our current cultural climate. A *New York Times* report in January 2007 described the "slow leak" of "young people who are falling away from the faith" that churches of all denominations are encountering.

"Mainline Christian churches have grappled with the problem for years. And recently evangelical leaders in the United States have sounded an alarm over 'an epidemic of young people leaving.'"[28] There are countertrends as well, and in the adult population at large, religious faith has held fairly steady over the past few decades. But for this potential source of youth purpose, observers describe a new kind of "generation gap," in which many parents have been unwilling or unable to pass on their religious faith to their children.[29]

REALISM AND THE LARGER GOOD

Unfortunately, few young people today go about their preparation for adult life with the combination of self-appraisal and purposeful intent that produces a sense of calling. A sense of calling (as we shall see in chapter 4) requires (1) a realistic awareness of one's own abilities; (2) an interest in how those abilities can serve some aspect of the world's needs; and (3) a feeling of enjoyment in using one's abilities in this way. These rules can be applied to any occupation.

But many young people today are nowhere near achieving the integration of self-knowledge and purposeful service required. Many are simply drifting, while others grasp for some romantic fantasy career without any clear idea of what it would take to pursue it or anyone in their lives who is offering them help in such a quest. Many young people today harbor wildly unrealistic ambitions that bear little relation to their own abilities: moderately talented high school athletes who dream of becoming Michael Jordan, amateur film buffs who imagine themselves the next Steven Spielberg, high school newspaper reporters who see themselves going straight to the anchor job at a major TV network. A few of today's young people, no doubt, will have the talent, fire, and determination to make it in such celebrity careers. But most will have to grapple with the reality that they aren't cut out for those fields.

The root of the problem is that, while thinking about their future work, they consider only surface features of the vocation: what's in it for them, whether or not the work seems like it will capture their interest, the possibilities of fame and fortune, without considering what they are trying to accomplish and how their own particular aptitudes could be of use to the world beyond the self.

Successful people focus on what they are trying to achieve, and try to succeed in something that they know they can do; with this in mind, they know they will find the work interesting and meaningful. For a young person anticipating a career, purpose is the key to this all-important attitude. But where in our educational system do we introduce this crucial concept to our students? And when do we spend the time and effort to help our students match their abilities and interests with particular job choices (or even, in economic language, with the demands of the labor marketplace)? Too many young people are left to their own devices with respect to some of life's largest questions: What is my calling? What do I have to contribute to the world? What am I here for? It is as if we are running away from these questions, apprehensive about facing them, either for ourselves or for our children.

How some people make the right choices, and how adults in their lives can provide the kind of support and guidance that help them do so, are the subjects of the rest of this book. Our research shows how young people across the United States are struggling with this challenge, some successfully, others not; and I shall discuss the part that adult influences play in the resolution of these struggles. Then I offer my own recommendations as to how to raise children in a way that facilitates their attempts to find genuine purpose.

3

Who Is Thriving and Who Is Not Yet on Course?

In today's fractured world, the population of young people is sharply divided into separate groups, each moving at its own pace along its own particular developmental track. Some young people, with impressive skill and determination, are barreling down well-defined tracks toward auspicious destinations. Others are moving gradually and tentatively along tracks with destinations that they barely perceive. They are often uncertain about whether they are moving forward or backward, and they may or may not keep moving in a positive direction. Still others seem content to stay pretty much as they are, not worrying about whether they are on any track; though "content" may be the wrong word for their apathy. And, a deeply troubled group of young people today are heading down tracks toward self-destruction, or violence toward others. In order to help children become more purposeful, it is helpful to know what kind of direction they have taken thus far in their lives.

These distinct groups tend to socialize separately, and they exhibit markedly different styles and attitudes about their world and their aspirations. It is therefore misleading and inaccurate to describe "today's youth" in general terms. There is one general point, however, that must be made about our population: virtually all young people need more attention and guidance from their elders than they are currently receiving. I am not referring here to the micromanaging of the widely noted "helicopter parent" but to something that is both deeper and less intrusive, as I shall discuss in chapter 6.

In this chapter I draw on the first of a series of studies of youth development that my students and I have been carrying out over the past seven years in order to profile these distinct groups and their attitudes. These studies were national in scope, with data collected from five communities scattered across the United States: an inner-city urban community on the east coast; an affluent suburb on the west coast; a small southern town; and two heterogeneous cities in the midst of agricultural regions.[1]

Since 2003, we have surveyed over twelve hundred young people between the ages of twelve and twenty-six, and we have interviewed in depth approximately a quarter of those surveyed.[2] Our surveys first ask young people to indicate if, where, and in what way they have found purpose in their lives. The interviews then probe into these issues in greater depth, asking why the person believes that a stated activity or goal is meaningful, what the person hopes to accomplish in life, now and in the future, and what kinds of life choices the person has made so far. (Our youth purpose interview appears in the Appendix at the end of this book.)

In this chapter, based on the initial study that we completed in 2006, I will draw a portrait of how today's youth are finding—or not finding—purpose in their lives. The overall picture is, I believe, disconcerting enough (with some striking exceptions); yet it is not complete. Our own studies cannot offer access to the minds and feelings of those young people who are seriously disturbed and pose threats to themselves and others. For one thing, such people do not usually sign up for probing studies like ours, and of course participation in our studies is always voluntary. Moreover, our instruments are geared to elicit positive sentiments—young people's hopes and aspirations, what matters to them and why, what they find inspiring and motivating. By its very nature, our research method is not sensitive to the darker and angrier sentiments harbored by people who commit acts of violence. I am not at all sure that, even if a hate-filled youngster were to wander into one of our interview sessions, we would be able to detect from our questions the full danger lurking in that child's heart.

Any truly complete account of youth purpose, and its absence, should however take account of both normal and abnormal, even antisocial, behavior that may on its surface appear to have qualities similar to purpose. In order to address the question of abnormal and harmful "purpose," therefore, I will draw on a pair of sources beyond my own studies: an official British government report on the suicide bombings that took place in London during 2005; and an in-depth account of the 1998 Columbine High School shootings in Littleton, Colorado. In both cases, there is enough information for us to discern the workings of purpose, or its lack, in the minds of young people who are bent on destruction.

SOURCES OF YOUTH PURPOSE

Although, as I've said, generalizing about the dispositions of today's young people misses vital distinctions among their groupings, I do think that before profiling the distinct groups, it is enlightening to take a look at the collective results of our interviews in one regard.[3] One of the things we were concerned with was to discover what were the most important sources of purpose today for those young people who expressed any sense of purpose at all. Doing so produced some informative results, and these results point the way, I believe, to areas in which we can be encouraging our young people—all of our young people—to engage in activities that they will find meaningful.

For the following analysis, Jennifer Menon Mariano and I examined young people's responses to the following instruction: *We are interested in finding out what types of things you feel are most important to you, based on how much time and energy you commit to them. For the following items, please circle the number that corresponds to how dedicated you are.* This instruction was followed by a list of eighteen categories, some of which were nonpurposeful and mainly self-oriented ("looking good," "money," "growth," "happiness") and some of which reflected some degree of purpose beyond the self ("family," "career," "faith," "community service," and so on). We then calculated a "dedication" average for all of the purposeful and nonpurposeful categories, to determine the degree to which each category was attracting the time and energy commitments of our young subjects. The young people who took this survey in our study expressed dedication to the purposeful categories in the following descending order, with family as their top concern and political and societal issues as the least of their interests:

- Family
- Career
- Academic achievement
- Religious faith or spirituality
- Sports
- Arts
- Community service
- Political/societal issues

We see that family is first among sources of purpose for today's youth. For some young people, this simply means remaining close to, and possibly caring for, the family that raised them. Others see their ultimate aim as creating and nurturing a family of their own. For these young people, all their other goals—graduating from school, getting a job, finding a home of their own—are directed toward establishing their own family.

Should it surprise us that so many young people look to family as the first source of meaning in their lives? Perhaps this number would not seem so startling if old stereotypes about girls and women were true. If girls were still raised to view themselves primarily as family caregivers, we might expect that this half of the population would focus their search for purpose on the realm of family. But such stereotypes are long obsolete, at least in nontraditional societies; and in fact in our studies we found no gender differences between boys and girls in their designations of family as a source of purpose.

What this finding does reveal is that young people today—boys and girls alike—feel connected to their families in ways that eluded many in the generations that immediately preceded them. This sense of connectedness underlies the frequent and intimate communications between today's grown children and their parents that I referred to earlier.

The relatively small proportion who name dedication to faith as a source of purpose may be in line with prior research on religiosity among the young. One landmark investigation of American youth, conducted over twenty-five years ago, in the 1980s, found that 15 percent of its participants were devoutly faithful, suggesting that they considered serving God to be their ultimate concern.[4] It appears that this percentage of highly religious youth has remained fairly stable nationwide over the past few decades; but whether that will remain true, in light of the more recent declines that I noted in chapter 2, is another question.

Interestingly, in the 1980s study, religiosity was found to play a distinctively positive role in healthy development. The study identified many negative factors that predicted problems in development, such as abusive parents, alcoholism or drug addiction in the family, and biogenetic or psychological disorders; but religiosity was alone among the positive factors (such as high IQ, family wealth, and social popularity) that significantly predicted successful adaptation during youth. This finding speaks to the power of faith-based purpose to direct lives in positive directions, at least for those young people who become truly devout in their faith. In making this point, it is important to note, however, that this twenty-five-year-old study did not try to measure the role of such factors as hopes, expectations, stated aspirations, or secular beliefs, which I would argue would also have been shown to predict positive development had they been included.

Of the less frequent contemporary sources of purpose, the one that is most noteworthy in its low ranking in our survey is political and societal interest. Few young people today imagine that they might find purpose in the public sphere as politicians, civic leaders, or community organizers. There is very little public leadership aspiration among today's younger generation. In fact, there may never have been a time in American history when so small a proportion of the population aged twenty to thirty have sought or accepted leadership roles in local civic organizations. Not only are young people today not interested in such roles, but it is hard to find a public figure on any level (other than in sports and entertainment) that the young admire, let alone wish to emulate. In fact, many of today's young show little interest in society beyond the tight circle of their family and immediate friends. This lack of interest can be seen in the state of their civic knowledge. In a U.S. Department of Education assessment a few years ago, only 9 percent of high school students were able to cite reasons why it is important for citizens to participate in a democracy, and only 6 percent could identify some reasons why having a constitution benefits a country.[5] This decline in political engagement has been well documented in other surveys as well. For example, one study showed that, from 1966 to 2002, interest in political affairs among college freshmen declined in a steady stepwise fashion *by over half*, from 60 percent of the population to less than 30 percent.[6]

We have also seen this disturbing trend in our own prior research on youth attitudes for almost a decade now. In one study a few years ago, we collected in-depth interviews with young people living in heartland American communities, and we also examined essays that hundreds of other students had written about the laws and purpose of life in today's world.[7] What struck us was not only what these young people said but what they did *not* say. They showed little awareness of current events and voiced virtually no expression of social concern, political opinion, civic duty, patriotic emotion, or sense of citizenship in any form.

When asked what American citizenship meant to him, one student replied, "We just had that the other day in history. I forget what it was." Another said, "I mean, being American is not really special. . . . I don't find being an American citizen very important"; and another, "I don't know, I figure everybody is a citizen so it really shouldn't mean nothing." One student said, directly: "I don't want to belong to any country. It just feels like you are obligated to this country. I don't like the whole thing of citizen . . . I don't like that whole thing. It's like, citizen, no citizen, it doesn't make sense to me. It's, like, to be a good citizen, I don't know. I don't want to be a citizen . . . it's stupid to me." Such statements, of course, are not universal: there are some young people who dedicate themselves to their country with strong feelings of civic commitment. But they are more the exception than the rule.

As for the idea of a career in politics, it is generally viewed with suspicion and distaste. "Most [politicians] . . . are kind of crooked," one of our interviewees declared. Another student, also showing typical attitudes when asked about national politics, said, "I feel like one person can't do that much and . . . I get the impression that [most people] don't think a group of people can do that much." The cynicism expressed carried over to political action at all levels, including even school. When talking about how school government works, one girl said, "The principal and vice principals probably make the decisions and say what is going on and don't worry about it." A palpable feeling of futility—a "what's the use?" sensibility—runs through most students' attitudes about political participation.

Although some of the people in our study considered themselves to be leaders among their friends, almost none desired to be a civic or political leader (there was a lone exception in our sample). One boy dismissed the idea by saying, "It just doesn't seem like a very good job to me. I'd rather be concentrating on more artistic efforts rather than civic efforts or saving the world or something."

Is this unusual, or remarkable in any way? Hasn't youth always been a time for the pursuit of personal pleasures and intimate relationships rather than participation in the broader civil society? Have the young ever been driven by a sense of civic duty or dedicated to social and political purposes beyond their own everyday lives? Indeed, is there not plenty of time in later life to get interested in such things?

The uncomfortable answers to these questions are: (1) Yes, young people's present lack of dedication to broader civil purposes is unusual by any historical standards that we have. (2) No, youth traditionally has not been a time of exclusively personal goals to the exclusion of civic ones. And (3) many young people normally have been drawn to civic and political affairs by their late adolescence. In fact, there is reason to believe that a person's crucial orientations to life incubate during adolescence. If civic concern is not among them, it may never arise.

We all have memories, of course, of times in our own recent history when young people in large numbers threw themselves into the political fray. They joined the civil rights movement, campaigned for political candidates, lobbied for environmental protection, and protested government actions that they did not like, such as the Vietnam War and the Watergate scandals. That dedication was also carried through to later life for many. One late twentieth-century sociological study showed that young people who marched for civil rights in the 1960s were far more likely than their peers to later join civil associations, assume positions of civic leadership, and vote.[8]

All this raises warning flags for the future of our democratic republic. As the legendary educator Robert Maynard Hutchins once wrote, "The death of democracy is not likely to be an assassination from ambush. It will be a slow extinction from apathy, indifference and undernourishment." It also is of grave concern to those who believe, as I do, that a strong sense of citizenship is an essential part of a fully developed personality. Virtually all theories of human development portray adolescence as a period when young people formulate their identities. The civic component of an identity is an allegiance to a systematic set of moral and social beliefs, a kind of personal ideology, to which a young person stakes out a commitment. The particular commitment, of course, may change over subsequent years with maturity and experience; but its initial formulation during adolescence is a key milestone of human development. A budding civic identity becomes the basis for a dedication to community and, eventually, to the broader society. If such purposeful dedication is slipping away over the generations, both the future public good and the personal well-being of our developing youth stand at risk.

By way of an overall conclusion about these findings, I would venture that while the strong sense of purpose expressed by a good number of today's young people in family life is wonderful, the fact that so few report that they find similar meaning in their work and civic life is troubling. It is vital, I would argue, that adults find ways to inspire more excitement about these pursuits, for, as we will see in profiling the most highly motivated youngsters we studied in more depth, *every single one of them* found significant meaning in these areas of life.

THE DISENGAGED, THE DREAMERS, THE DABBLERS, AND THE PURPOSEFUL

So, how do today's youth divide in terms of the sense of purpose they express in their lives? As we've seen, our initial national sample of young people broke down into four groups, which I shall call the *disengaged* and nonpurposeful, the *dreamers*, the *dabblers*, and the *purposeful*.

In brief, the *disengaged* are those young people who expressed no purpose at all in our surveys or interviews. They are not active in any endeavor that might turn into a purposeful pursuit; nor do they show signs that they are looking to find such pursuits. Some in this group are apathetic and detached; others confine their interests to hedonic or ego-boosting pursuits that show little concern for the world beyond the self.

The *dreamers* are those who express ideas about purposes that they would like to have—sometimes stirring and imaginative ideas—but who have done little or nothing actively to try out any of their ideas. They have idealistic aspirations and can imagine doing great things in the world. But thus far they have done little to put their ideas to the test of action. As a result, these young people have not developed the practical plans needed for pursuing their purpose in a realistic way.

The *dabblers* are youth who have engaged in activities that appear to be at least potentially purposeful, but who showed little awareness of the meaning of these activities beyond the present; consequently, these young people show few signs of committing themselves to these pursuits over time. They often skip from one activity to the next without any coherent sense of what they wish to accomplish in their lives. They may have tried out a number of engaging pursuits—indeed, in some cases too many to keep track of—but they have yet to find a compelling reason to sustain a commitment to any one of them. Their interests are too tentative and too fleeting to become the basis of an enduring personal identity.

The *purposeful* are those who have found something meaningful to dedicate themselves to, who have sustained this interest over a period of time, and who express a clear sense of what they are trying to accomplish in the world and why. They have found a cause or ultimate goal that inspires their efforts from day to day and helps them fashion a coherent future agenda. They know what they want to accomplish and why, and they have taken concerted steps to achieve their ambitions.

According to the results of our first study, 20 percent of the young people we interviewed were purposeful in the full sense that I described above. At the other extreme, we found 25 percent to be disengaged, expressing virtually no purpose and showing no signs of seeking anything remotely purposeful. Approximately another 25 percent we found to be *dreamers*, who have purposeful aspirations but have taken few if any steps to act upon those aspirations. And approximately 31 percent we found to be *dabblers*, who have actively tried out a number of potentially purposeful pursuits, but without a clear sense of why they are doing so or whether they will sustain these interests into the future. These percentages add to 101 percent because of rounding.

It is the dreamers and the dabblers who seem to be in the greatest state of developmental flux. Those in these groups may, in their own ways, be moving toward something that will give their lives meaning. Or they may remain frozen in place, if their paths do not lead them to a cause or engagement that captures their energy and imagination. Together, these two groups comprise the majority of the youth population, and so the stakes of their eventual journeys are especially high. Our responsibility as adults to help them in their early tentative steps should be clear to all of us.

In order to provide a more detailed picture of how the youth in these groups think and sound, of the ways they reveal their lack of purpose, and how we can figure out where a given young person is in this terrain, the portraits below draw on particular young people from our study. Their statements are reported verbatim, though I have changed their names and some incidental details to protect their privacy.

The Disengaged and the Nonpurposeful

In chapter 1, I quoted two teenagers who responded to our interviews with clear expressions of disengagement. One of the boys disclaimed having any long-term goals, and the other celebrated his "let-the-chips-fall-where-they-may" orientation to the future. Each boy in his own way had consciously accepted apathy as part of his approach to life.

Most nonpurposeful young people are neither as articulate nor as aware of their sense of disengagement as these two boys. The nonpurposeful young people in our study usually responded to our questions about purpose with blank looks or with statements such as "I don't know, I haven't thought about it that much." Few accept their disengagement as confidently as these two boys: most do not seem convinced that apathy and laziness are "all right." Yet many disengaged youth do share a sense that *drift* is a reasonable way of getting through life. Some accept drifting as inevitable ("you can't control the future, so why bother?"), while others see it as a fine way to "have a good time." In fact, for many of these youth, having a good time is the closest thing they have to an abiding goal. They may express some interest in getting a degree, finding a job, earning a lot of money, or having a family; but they see such objectives as little more than ways of getting through life with as little pain and as much pleasure as possible. For some, this means no more than "getting with the program" that others present to them as necessary for adaptation. In the end, this leaves them guided by little more than concerns of survival ("getting by from day to day") or hedonism ("having fun"), rather than by aspirations of genuine accomplishment or personal fulfillment.

For example, when one boy was asked how he would like to be remembered, he said: "Fun . . . a fun person. People like fun people. They're cool to be around. I just want to be remembered as cool." When asked about his future, the boy said: "I don't try to have long-term goals. I don't think too far in the future. It's not important to have goals." When asked what it would mean for him to have a good life, he simply said: "A good life is when you, like, do things to make you happy. As long as I'm happy I feel like I have a good life. Once I'm not happy, then it's not the good life anymore." He did note a number of potentially constructive activities that he was doing from day to day, such as going to school and making friends; but none of these activities had any meaning for him unless he found it to be fun. On this account, he had no reason to commit to any of them or to any other engagements beyond the moment.

A twenty-year-old young woman we interviewed saw her life as a series of events with no organizing plans or deeper principles: "Every day turns, every day it's going to be something new. It's kind of like a new book, every day turns like a new page, so each page is not going to be the same, it's going to be something different." During the interview, she expressed two abiding concerns: making friends and losing weight. Both concerns seemed to be driven only by hedonistic desires (making friends in order to have fun and losing weight in order to look good). She stated that she believed it important to finish college "because at least graduating college with a four-year degree, it allows me or anyone just to do almost anything. Having a degree, any degree, it looks good . . . it [enables you] to make more money, be happy, buy a Ferrari or something. Take the cruise, like a 14-day cruise or something, spend the $12,000 and think, oh, it's nothing, whatever." She spoke of a large number of disparate career possibilities, but she had no basis for choosing among them, because none of her concerns addressed the questions of what she wished to accomplish and why. Her desires to make friends, look good, and make money did not provide her with much direction when it came to formulating a plan for the future to which she could dedicate herself.

From my perspective as both a researcher and an educator, this disengaged group poses by far the greatest challenge for parents and educators. The particular problem these young people present in a research sense lies in understanding what, if any, hidden feelings they may have below the veneer of cynicism revealed in their interviews. Is their bravado, or their nonchalance, genuine? Or is it a cover for feelings of anguish and self-doubt? Would deeper probing reveal goals that they are not prepared to talk about in public?

As we move forward with our research over the coming years, one of our main priorities will be to learn more about this disturbingly large group of disengaged youngsters. The challenge of working with disengaged youth also must be a top educational priority. Unlike the rest of the youth population, the disengaged seem to offer no place to start. If they are not even looking for purpose—indeed, if they are hostile to any goals at all beyond day-to-day pleasures—how can we help them find a direction to guide their lives? I have struggled with this question and frequently ask people with experience and wisdom for their counsel on it.[9] The consensus answer I have received is that we must find ways to bring home to these youngsters the unhappiness that a life without purpose will lead to, and, on the upside, the fulfillment that commitment to a purpose provides. In chapters 5–7 we will revisit this difficult issue in more detail.

The Dreamers

Sara is a bright and high-achieving college student. By her junior year in college, she has received a broad liberal arts education with a major in English literature. Sara has a wide range of interests in and out of the classroom. She is well informed about current events and cultural trends, and has an active social life, with many friends. She loves film and theater, occasionally taking leading roles in school drama productions.

Sara frequently expresses idealistic impulses about her desire to make the world a better place. Sometimes these impulses, though they seem to be sincerely felt, are somewhat unfocused, as when she says: "I want to do something good. I want to change the world for the better, because I'm so worried about the world around me. I want to make a difference." Other times her aspirations begin to take on a focus related to her interest in film: "I want to make important movies, like, I want to make a documentary about the double standards that girls and women face." But apart from participating in student theater performances and an amateur video production, Sara has done little to prepare herself for a serious career that could turn her dreams into a reality. Nowhere does she indicate an understanding that succeeding in the highly competitive film world requires an extraordinary amount of training and hard work; nor has she taken any steps to acquire such training or experience.

In this area of interest and aspiration, Sara has a lot of company. There is a legion of top students today who dream of becoming media stars in film, theater, television, or one of the performing arts. Few will realize their dreams, in part because there is not enough demand to place all of them in professional media careers, but also because not many of them have a grasp of the practical requirements of this career path. They have developed their interest in the area more as consumers who have been moved and entertained by productions that inspired them than as students and workers who must go through the hard process of learning in order to acquire the skills to achieve on their own. Few are prepared for the long, uncertain, and frustrating road they will need to travel if they are to even get a chance to try out their own ideas. A number of high-profile careers attract dreamers—sports, high finance, space travel, poetry—but in our time entertainment is front and center in the minds of many of the best and brightest among our young people. Some, even among the dreamers, will learn to go about it in the right way; but this will require a commitment that goes beyond what Sara and others in her group have been able to express thus far.

Then there is the subset of dreamers who have yet to find even an unrealistic focus for their aspirations, such as Jimmy, age seventeen, a high school senior from an affluent west coast suburb. Jimmy's sentiments are admirably earnest and well-meaning, yet hard to bring down to earth: "I really think it's so important to become more aware of what happens around you and to become more connected to the trees and the floor . . . all these abstract things that are actually very connected. And nonviolence, because here there's so much violence, and not just in an abstract way." Jimmy, like others in this group, will need to forge his ideals on the anvil of experience before they take on the shape of a true purpose.

The Dabblers

Robert, a seventeen-year-old, is optimistic about his future and has some solid ideas about the path he would like to pursue. He says that after high school, "I'm planning on going into the military to be an intelligence officer." After that, "I want to work for the government. . . . Lots of people who work for the government are ex-military—I want to try for FBI or CIA." Robert has worked hard to get the grades he will need to graduate and join the military, and he has considered what his military service can prepare him for in a careful and intelligent manner. Insofar as it is possible to predict anything about the future of a seventeen-year-old, Robert seems to be headed for a secure and promising career trajectory. He has somewhat more direction than many of those whom we categorized as "dabblers."

The main thing that is shaky about Robert's plans is his understanding of what he will be accomplishing in military or government service. His focus is confined to the perquisites and other external trappings of these jobs rather than the significance of the actual work he will be doing. Robert's main reason for choosing this career path is that "it's got prestige that comes with it and you can just say that you've got a real good job." The other reason he gives is that "the military offers me a chance to see the world. I've always wanted to go overseas and I've never been able to."

In a personal sense, Robert's reasons may be perfectly valid; but for the sake of his professional motivation and achievement, he eventually will need to develop a deeper sense of what he is doing and why. At this point, his images of the career he has chosen are romanticized in an almost fairy-tale fashion: "Strength and honor," he says, when asked what inspires him about military service. "It's kind of like a Middle Ages knight." His image of a government career—the future he hopes military service will lead him to—is even less well defined. Robert describes his aspirations for this career as follows: "Hopefully I'll be back in the States behind a desk, safe" . . . and "I'll probably stay the 20 (years) and retire. . . . Just be prosperous at the same time."

Robert may be in a state of transition toward a purposeful future. He has a good plan for a rewarding vocation, and in many respects his thinking is realistic and sensible. For example, he reasons that "the military is really going to teach me everything I need to know about basic skills and basic understanding of computers and stuff like that." He also knows that "the path I've chosen requires a lot of a person, a lot of their time," and he has shown through his record of school achievement that he is ready to deliver on this responsibility. What's more, when discussing his views on citizenship, Robert shows recognition of some of the military's positive contributions to society, referring to the importance of "being protected." His views on this are still rudimentary and unconnected with his own vision of what he might accomplish in the service; but they may offer him the beginnings of a more mature conception of how he might make his own contribution someday. Also a good sign, Robert, like most youngsters, hopes to have a life of consequence—or as he put it in his own words, "make my little mark on the planet."

Robert is still a seeker, because he has not quite found the intrinsic purpose in the work that he aspires to do. His focus on such goals as prestige and travel, and his unrealistic ideas about military life, give his interests something of a "dabbling" quality. If he is to find that work meaningful and personally fulfilling over the long haul—indeed, if he is to devote himself wholeheartedly to that work and excel at it—Robert will need to discover that purpose.

The Purposeful

Casey is a twenty-year-old college student from a rural area in the Midwest. Raised in a nonaffluent family, she has had odd jobs since she was fourteen, and recently became a part-time manager of a local coffee bar. Casey's career aspiration is to become a history teacher, and she is clearly purposeful in her orientation to the vocation of teaching. But Casey's primary purpose is family, followed by her faith. Her work goals are important to her; yet she sees them as just part of the multiple purposes she has found for her life.

Speaking of her priorities, Casey says: "My family is top priority to me. . . . We've always been real close. . . . I just want to pass on the stuff that my dad taught me, showed me, I want to pass it along to my children and keep it going, keep the tradition of the family going on."

Church is also one of her priorities, but, she says, "church isn't as important to me as it is to the rest of my family." Casey, however, sees faith as providing a significant part of the meaning of work: "The Bible says that work without faith is nothing. If you don't have faith then you're not going to get anywhere . . . it kind of gave me a direction and a goal to go towards, and that helped me out a lot."

As for Casey's work plans, they are conceived with a sharp sense of mission: "I want to teach. I want to be the best teacher I can be. Teaching is not a nine-to-five job. It's a lifestyle, not a job. It's something you have to have in you to do." Casey's desire to teach history stems from her dissatisfaction with the way history is now taught in schools, and she has a reformer's zeal about her determination to change that: "You can't find a history teacher that actually just wants to teach. They all just sit there and [say] read chapter one, do this worksheet, have it in by Friday. It's not teaching anyone. You have to make it interesting. . . . That's one reason I want to teach history. I love it so much . . . and if you actually make it fun, they'll learn."

Some purposeful youngsters have one burning purpose, focusing on a particular concern related to their family, faith, work, or community aspirations. Others, like Casey, have acquired purposes across several of these fronts. In some cases, the purposes may be nested and prioritized: My work is meaningful, but in the end the most important thing is that it enables me to provide for my family; or, I want to have a close family so that I will have the stability to get my work done; or, I love and care for my family, which is a main part of my efforts to be a good citizen and build a strong community; or, I wish to do any or all of the above as my way of serving God. In other cases, the purposes may coexist as a kind of parallel list, equally important and not really intersecting with one another. A purpose also may evolve into a new or expanded concern as, for example, when a young person who loves computer programming develops an interest in organizing a business in software technology. Although purposes are relatively stable affairs requiring long-term commitment, this does not mean that they remain frozen forever. Youth in particular is a dynamic period, and it is common for young people to combine and recombine their purposes as they learn more about themselves and the nature of their own ultimate concerns.

Also in this group of the clearly purposeful are a few youngsters who are truly extraordinary in the strength of their commitments and the extent to which they have already achieved impressive accomplishments. Some still in their midteens are already making a difference in their communities and, in some cases, in the world beyond. They are raising money for charitable causes, lobbying for social change, starting small businesses, experimenting with new forms of music, art, and computer technology, practicing their religious faith, exhibiting entrepreneurship, and working to advance any number of noble causes. Although their activities are far from the norm, their lives in many ways are indistinguishable from those of other thriving adolescents. We have a lot to learn from their early successes.

The Deeply Disturbed

No treatment of human purpose would be complete without a frank discussion of the malevolent forms that purpose can take when detached from its moral and ethical moorings. It is tragically the case that some people who appear to be driven by "purpose" can cause horrendous damage to themselves and others. To be sure, there are crucial differences between the antisocial "purposes" that some misguided people pursue and the purposes that inspire people toward positive ends. But there are similarities in the two kinds of purpose—pro- and antisocial—as well, especially with respect to the kinds of energy and passion that they can trigger in young people. Because significant numbers of apparently purposeful youngsters are engaging in deeds of massive destruction these days, with no letup in sight, it is urgent for us to try to understand everything we can about what motivates their behavior, and how to identify this breed of misdirected purpose.

Every case of violence has its own particular circumstances. Malevolent acts during youth usually are caused by multiple factors. A full explanation of such behavior requires a treatment of all the social and psychological issues that may be involved. I shall not attempt that kind of full treatment here. Rather, I shall focus on the role that a misguided sense of purpose can play, with the acknowledgment that other maladaptive social and psychological processes also may contribute to any such incident.

On July 7, 2005, four coordinated bombings devastated the London public transit system. The first three bombs hit three trains in the Underground (or subway) pretty much simultaneously, and the fourth bomb exploded on a double-decker bus an hour later. The attacks killed fifty-six passengers and wounded almost seven hundred others. The British government has identified four young men—one aged eighteen, one nineteen, one twenty-two, and one thirty—as perpetrators of the attacks. All four died in the bombings. But in an insightful official report, the British House of Commons provides a glimpse into the minds of these four young men.[10]

One striking, even chilling, observation is that their backgrounds "appear largely unexceptional." The formative experiences that had shaped their early lives seemed indistinguishable from those of their peers; and much of their behavior prior to the bombings appeared to be reasonably well adjusted. The oldest of the four, whom the report identified as the ringleader, was remembered to be "quiet, studious and never in trouble." One of the others "did well academically and was a gifted sportsman"; at school, this boy was remembered as "calm, friendly, mature, and modest, and was popular with his peers." A third was "a bright child, successful academically at school and good at sport." Indeed, all of them played sports avidly and participated in such outward-bound-type activities as canoeing, whitewater rafting, and camping trips, all of which normally can be part of a wholesome lifestyle for young people.

But their lives also contained some disturbing elements, outside the range of the ordinary. The report comments that "there was a subtle change in [the ringleader's] character . . . he is said to have become less talkative and more introverted. On a couple of occasions, he showed uncharacteristic intolerance out of line with his normally easygoing manner." His intolerance was based upon extremist views that had begun to influence him and each of the other three young men. On the eve of their actions, as the men became increasingly swept up in the fervor of these extremist views, they produced video-taped expressions of the ideas that were driving them. Their statements are at once wildly idealistic and grimly otherworldly, as in: "Our driving motivation doesn't come from tangible commodities that this world has to offer . . . but obedience to the one true God"; and: "We love death the way you love life."[11] The latter statement is a reference to the value of martyrdom, which according to the report is at the center of the ideology that was motivating these young men.

It cannot be denied that "the driving motivation" experienced by such young men has some things in common with the sentiments expressed by young people who dedicate themselves to pro-social purposes. The professed motives of the young Englishmen were emblematic in that they demonstrated *an intense commitment to their ideals; a burning desire to "make a difference" in the world; an intention to redress a perceived injustice*; and *spiritual beliefs that supported and guided their commitments*. Moreover, these misguided young people, much like those who are highly dedicated to pro-social purposes, *sustained their commitments over extended periods of time* and *engaged in long-term planning to accomplish their missions*. Finally, these young men were *strongly influenced by the examples and advocacies of adult mentors* whom they admired and emulated, again much like highly purposeful pro-social youth. In all these ways, young people with antisocial or pro-social purposes have qualities in common that are not shared by less purposeful youth.

The great difference between the two types lies in the contrasting nature of their adopted purposes. The purposes of pro-social youth are life-affirming, and they do not celebrate death or destruction. Nor do pro-social young people assume that violence is a legitimate means of pursuing an end, however noble; and they do not treat the lives of others as expendable in the pursuit of such ends. Instead, they see other people's lives as ends in themselves that must be protected. As for their own lives, they are fully prepared to dedicate them wholeheartedly to their chosen purposes; but they wish to achieve their goals not by dying, but by *living* in a manner that fulfills their sense of who they are and want to be—that is, in a manner consistent with their recently forged personal identities.

On April 20, 1999, on the other side of the Atlantic, two teenage boys, Eric Harris and Dylan Klebold, massacred twelve schoolmates and a teacher in the infamous Columbine High School shootings. These two boys were dissimilar in many ways from the London suicide bombers, with sharply different psychological characteristics and ideological beliefs. But certain things they had in common: a burning desire to make a difference in the world; a celebration of death; a sense of spiritual validation for their actions; a capacity to sustain their determination for long periods of time; an ability to put their long-term plans into action; and a tendency to be influenced by prior examples. In his diary/notebook, one of the boys wrote: "I want to make a lasting impression on the world."[12] The other, in a "last will," wrote: "What fun is life without a little death?"

Harris and Klebold left over nine hundred pages of documents that detailed their grievances and plans for revenge. In addition, they created Web sites and videos announcing grandiose sentiments such as "We're going to kick-start a revolution of the dispossessed."[13] Many of the documents date back to the year prior to the killings, and there is evidence that the boys engaged in a significant amount of long-term planning for the atrocity. They quoted extensively from classic literature; and in their final hours before the shootings, they taped themselves speaking about references with religious meaning, such as Judgment Day and the Apocalypse.

If these boys had been pursuing pro-social goals, all their energy, planning, and eager persistence would appear to us as perfectly characteristic of young people inspired by noble purposes. Of course, these boys no doubt were disturbed in many ways, and their antisocial sense of purpose arose in the context of these disturbances. Over the years, as experts examine the trove of documents that these tragically intelligent boys left behind, more will be known about the state of their mental health as they planned and committed the massacre. For now, we must conclude that, for all the apparent commonalities between pro- and antisocial purposes, they differ in so many fundamental ways that they really cannot be spoken about in the same breath. Such purposes originate in radically opposing visions about how to "make a difference" in the world, and they contrast sharply in their assumptions about how other people should be treated. Most importantly, pro-social purposes affirm life and conform to traditional moral, ethical, and legal standards; antisocial purposes celebrate death and ignore any standards that might get in the way of the malevolent intent.

There are many different ways that a young person can stray toward antisocial purpose, but one thing can be said in many such cases: that young person has not had sufficient opportunity to find a pro-social purpose that could preempt the lure of the antisocial one. Any vacuum, whether physical or psychological, will eventually be filled.[14] If we do not provide our young people with positive guidance to inspire their behavior, they may well seek guidance of a less positive sort. Clearly, when it comes to perceiving whether—and how—our children are developing a sense of purpose in their lives, all adults and educators must be on the lookout for any turn toward the antisocial.

Young people who find noble purposes are idealistic in an optimistic rather than an angry or self-aggrandizing way. They learn to translate their idealism into realism, but they do not turn their realism into cynicism or nihilism. They have no trouble avoiding macabre, self-destructive, and violent tendencies, because they have found purposes that inspire them and fill their lives with positive activity.

In our studies, we set out to describe the situation of young people today in terms of their discovery of purpose in life, but also to identify the key elements that make the difference for those who succeed. We wanted to put our fingers on what parents and the society at large can do to most effectively help young people get on the right path. To that end, we decided to interview in depth twelve young people whom we had identified as especially purposeful: youngsters who were strikingly motivated, engaged, happy, and deeply committed to some pursuit in which they found a great wealth of purpose. The results were gratifying: in every case, we were able to perceive a set of key common factors that had helped them. In the next chapter, we'll take a close look at those factors and the role they played, en route to articulating how the society is currently failing so many of our young people. We'll then look at how parents, and the other adults in young people's lives, can most effectively help them on their way.

4

Profiles in Purpose

The young people who form the minority-within-a-minority of the most highly purposeful are strongly motivated and extremely effective. They have succeeded, at this young age, in advancing their purposes in a manner that would be impressive for people several times older. For our study, we selected twelve boys and girls who had taken on major commitments to purposes and had stuck with them, often with enormous effect, for several years. We then interviewed them at length in order to obtain firsthand accounts of how each had discovered and pursued his or her own particular purpose. For all but one of the twelve, we also kept in touch with them and reinterviewed them two years later; and whenever possible, we asked their parents as well for information about their children's route to their purposeful paths.

Some of the pursuits of these twelve impressive young people are altruistic—for example, raising money to provide clean drinking water for families in Africa, or contributing to charitable organizations that aid cancer victims and conduct research that combats the disease. Others are involved in civic or political causes, such as lobbying for stronger gun control or environmental regulation, and rallying support for candidates with solutions for Mideast peace. Some are artistic or scientific quests—learning and creating new jazz music scales, or writing innovative computer software programs. Some of the youngsters are budding entrepreneurs; and two are junior missionaries, each promoting a different religious faith.

Our focus in this chapter will be on the stories of four of the twelve, with occasional examples from a few of the others, since the experiences of these young people serve well to represent consistent themes that arose in all of the interviews. As we look at their stories, and hear them describe in their own terms how purpose has so inspired and driven them, a number of vital lessons emerge about how purpose can be fashioned early in life.

In the duration and intensity of their dedication, these young people are clearly exceptional. Yet they convey an air of refreshing normalcy to those who know them: They go about their lives with a quiet but determined self-confidence, and they are self-motivated. With all they are doing, they rarely exude angst or frenzied stress. It may seem odd, even contradictory, to begin an introduction to twelve extraordinary young people by noting how normal they are in many ways (including, among other things, their family lives and the general way they were raised, their interests in friendships and enjoyable peer activities, their desire to carve out fitting places for themselves in the world, and their everyday demeanor). Many of them comment about this themselves, perhaps feeling they need to make the point amid all the recognition they get for their many achievements. "Just a normal kid" is a phrase frequently repeated in many of our interviews. One of the mothers, echoing her son's own description, told us, typically, that her son Ryan is "ordinary, normal in terms of what you expect from a child . . . I didn't do anything with him that I didn't do with my other kids. . . . He doesn't want to be special. He wants to fit in. He wants to make the hockey team . . . I mean, he's normal."

Indeed, this paradoxical normalcy is the first thing that struck us about these young people. Like most of their peers, given the chance to discuss their lives, they were open, outgoing, and talkative. They clearly enjoyed a chance to speak with adults who take their ideas seriously (an experience all too rare for young people in any society). Eager to reflect on their past experiences and future goals, they were also determinedly autonomous in their views, and not at all hesitant to criticize the way the world around them is being run. In fact, they seemed to draw extra energy, and a bit of irreverent glee, from expressing how appalled they are about conditions in the world that need changing. They are, in other words, normal adolescents who in many ways look and sound just like their peers.

The normalcy of these highly purposeful adolescents in look, bearing, and developmental viewpoint makes them of particular interest to us here. If these youngsters were some strangely evolved creatures who had little in common with any of their peers—for example, if they had IQs or physical skills that were off the charts—their stories might reveal little about how purpose can work in the daily lives of other youngsters. Music teachers trying to impart basic skills and musical appreciation to typical students will not find the most useful clues in a biography of Mozart. When it comes to a broad human quest of finding purpose, fortunately, there is more continuity between the ordinary and the extraordinary. Every person, however talented or gifted, has the capacity to find and make a sustained commitment to a purpose.[1] Moreover, the process of finding a purpose and dedicating oneself to it, and the personal benefits that follow from doing so, are also similar for all.

What *is* special about these highly motivated young people is their exceptional clarity of purpose. This clarity of purpose generates in them a prodigious amount of extra positive energy, which not only motivates them to pursue their goals passionately but also to acquire the skills and knowledge they need for this task. In the process, they become very good learners; and they develop a practical effectiveness unusual for people their age. They also reap a number of emotional benefits, such as self-confidence, optimism, gratitude, and a deep sense of personal fulfillment.

Ryan Hreljac was twelve years old when we first interviewed him and his mother. Already at that time, he had been working for six years to raise money for drinking wells in parts of rural Africa where families lacked sufficient water for daily living. His mother commented, almost in wonder, "He's been at this for six years. I don't know a whole lot of adults who have stuck with a project for six years." With help from his family, Ryan started a foundation, established a Web site (www.ryanswell.ca), and raised over $2 million to provide clean drinking water to households in fourteen developing countries in Africa and other parts of the world. For these remarkable efforts, Ryan has won numerous awards, including the World of Children Founder's Award, considered the equivalent of a Nobel Peace Prize for youth service.

Ryan found his purpose in first grade—astonishingly early even for highly purposeful youngsters. When his first-grade teacher told her class that children in Africa were dying because they couldn't get enough clean water to drink, Ryan became passionate about the idea of raising money to build drinking wells. He did extra chores around the house and saved $70, but he found that this formidable (to a six-year-old) sum of money didn't go very far toward solving the problem. Rather than get discouraged and give up, Ryan intensified his efforts. He collected funds from friends and people he knew and solicited further financial support from nonprofit organizations such as WaterCan, Free the Children, and Canadian Physicians for Aid and Relief. Before long, partly as a consequence of Ryan's efforts, wells and other clean water projects sprang up in many parts of Africa and other Third World countries. By 2007, the charitable foundation that Ryan and his family started—the Ryan's Well Foundation—had built 319 drinking wells in fourteen countries around the world. By that time, the foundation's Web site estimated that almost half a million people have gained better access to clean water as a result of the efforts of the foundation and those who have supported it. Yet, in the same spirit as that of the other highly purposeful youth we studied, the Web site quotes Ryan as saying, "I'm just your regular, average kid."

Amid all his awards and honors, Ryan's refusal to be self-aggrandizing is revealing. He shares with other highly purposeful youth a realistic perspective on his own contributions: Ryan is determined to make a difference in the world, but he does not see himself as unique or superior in this regard. "Anyone can do anything," he told us, "no matter who you are, no matter if you're a gas station clerk or the President of the United States." He believes that people should chip in to the best of their abilities, and everyone has a role to play: "You need to try to stand out and to do something for another person. Like, do something else to help somebody else, just little or small, just to help out." As for himself, Ryan intends to stretch: "I'm just going to go beyond my limits and see where I end up." This combination of ambition and realistic humility is one of the most distinct—and refreshing—marks of the highly purposeful young-sters we interviewed.

Whether this combination of ambition and realistic humility is a cause or effect of the effectiveness of these people is impossible to say; but it certainly is a central element in the character strength that enables them to tackle daunting challenges at such early ages. Making a positive difference in the world requires persistence (the problems that they care about are stubborn, or they would have already been solved) as well as optimism (it's easy to get discouraged when the problems remain despite your best efforts). Even as their ambition fuels their persistence, their realistic perspective about themselves keeps them optimistic in the face of inevitable setbacks. By recognizing their own (and everyone else's) limits, they resist harboring the kinds of inflated expectations that could lead them to discouragement.

Ryan's account of how he got started on his mission is a great case in point. He began with the misapprehension that saving $70 would do the trick. When he found out that the real cost of a single completed well was more like $2,000, he only intensified his efforts and adopted more elaborate strategies, confident that this persistence would eventually pay off:

So after four months of vacuuming, I raised $70. . . . And they told me, you know Ryan, it's going to take a lot more than $70 to build a well. $70 will only buy the hand pump to go on top. It will cost $2,000 to build the well. So when they told me that, I just said I would do more chores. Then when I got to around $100, I realized that I couldn't do this by vacuuming. So I started to do speeches and presentations. . . . It started to grow step by step. Then I raised $2,000 and kept on going. Then all these things happened. More stuff happened. I raised more money, and it just kept going to the next level.

The initial optimism that supported his persistence was fueled by the results he was able to achieve. In this way, there is a snowballing effect to such early character strengths as self-confidence, realistic humility, optimism, and persistence. These virtues are reinforced by the successes they lead to, and they become self-enforcing throughout development as the youngster discovers new ways to use his strengths to accomplish his purpose. This is why it is so important for parents to nurture such character strengths in their children from the start.

Although it is never too late for a child to acquire such strengths, starting early can afford a great advantage. There is strong continuity from childhood to later periods in life, and young people who have experienced a history of self-generated achievement have a unique opportunity to amplify these strengths in a cumulative way over many years of further growth.

It is important to stress that while the pursuit of purpose facilitates the development of character strengths such as optimism and self-confidence, it does not itself create those strengths. We know from recent brain and behavior research that character dispositions begin early in infancy and in some part may be inborn.[2] But these dispositions are susceptible to change all throughout development: for example, many severely inhibited youngsters lose their shyness by interacting positively with others during childhood.[3] Passionately pursuing a purpose directly engages young people in life experiences likely to enhance their optimism and self-confidence. For some, this means strengthening tendencies that are already there; for others, it means altering behavioral dispositions that lean in other directions. The latter cases also reveal that the pursuit of purpose does not depend upon any existing character disposition. Ryan, for example, was not always a highly self-confident child. "In my childhood," he told us, "I was a boy who was very sensitive. I cried over almost everything. I went to speech therapy because I stuttered. I didn't think I could ever be a leader." Now, after years of leadership in the cause that he believes in, Ryan is self-assured and forceful in his own quiet way.

When we interviewed him at age twelve, Ryan used eloquent metaphors as he spoke to us about the personal meaning of his own sense of purpose:

> Sometimes it's like you have a cup of tea or something. Most of us get poured too much and it overflows into our saucer. And some people just take that saucer and drink tea out of it. But what we should do is we should take that extra stuff and pour it in somebody else's cup who has so little.
>
> A life without a goal to do something, to make a difference, is like a race without a finish line. You can grow up, you can live a good life, you can do that, but maybe when you did get that house, maybe you could give back to the community to get that much farther in life.

Nina Vasan, at nineteen, had just started her second year at Harvard when we first interviewed her. As a student, Nina starred in several arenas: she played sports competitively, hosted her own radio show, received the $50,000 grand prize at the Intel International Science and Engineering Fair, presented her research during the Nobel Prize festivities, was named one of the top ten Girl Scouts in the nation, ran the Olympic torch, and was a pageant winner as West Virginia's Junior Miss. On top of all this, and most significantly, Nina founded and served as national president of American Cancer Society Teens, a nationwide network of teenagers working to support the ACS's mission through advocacy, education, fund-raising, and service. She initially started a teen group in her home state of West Virginia, then expanded it to include representation from all fifty states. ACS Teens encourages young people to become leaders in health through such activities as lobbying for smoke-free workplaces, writing educational literature on safe skin care, creating support groups for childhood cancer survivors, and raising money through all-youth Relays for Life.

Nina discovered her purpose when she was a young child. She recalls that as an eager and talkative five-year-old, she met a man whose voice box had been removed due to cancer. "I squinted my eyes," she recalls, "trying to make out the figure gradually approaching. A foreign hissing sound emanated continuously from the stranger. He slowly raised his trembling hand to cover the cavernous hole in his neck, and in an almost incomprehensible voice, muttered, 'Hehhyyoh.' Generally gregarious, I was stunned speechless. I later learned that this man, who was struggling to simply say 'Hello' to an impressionable child, smoked tobacco before society had adequately been educated about its dangers. While cancer robbed him of his speaking voice, the message he sent about smoking has shaped my life."

Witnessing firsthand these harsh realities of disease is the experience Nina credits with giving her a sense of purpose. She told us that after seeing the sobering effects of tobacco, as a little girl sporting pigtails and glasses two sizes too big, she would boldly tell strangers to "please stop smoking." It was this unabashed spirit that led to Nina's involvement with the American Cancer Society, as she searched for effective ways of making a difference.

One lesson that Nina came away with was how purpose can elevate and transform life: "This tobacco victim understood the importance of education in disease prevention, and he was trying to tell children his story as a way to educate them about the dangers of smoking. Reflecting back, I think that he found some purpose in his own life by trying to prevent others from suffering the same fate. He had hope and wanted to make sure his legacy would live on in others. It certainly worked, as he unknowingly helped me to find a sense of purpose in my own life."

Beyond this general lesson in living, Nina found a particular cause to dedicate herself to. She took on cancer prevention and cure, pursuing the cause in her own academic studies, which have concentrated in medicine and scientific research, as well as in the public policy arena, where she has campaigned for legislative and educational initiatives promoting cancer prevention and access to health care. And Nina's leadership was key to building a nationwide student network for the American Cancer Society. When she began this extraordinarily ambitious effort, Nina said, "teenagers had the interest and ability to impact the fight against cancer through methods beyond annual fund-raisers. As young people, we have a unique culture, mindset, and method of taking action. I thought that if we could unite and create a venue for students to realize their leadership potential, then we could be more effective in making long-lasting and comprehensive community change."

Nina did not do this alone. She found a mentor in a prominent local nurse and business leader who was in charge of an ACS-sponsored Daffodil Days fund-raiser. When the woman asked Nina to organize student volunteers for the event, the organization was overwhelmed to find that so many young people wanted to help. They ended up having to turn some away. In order to find a role for those interested, the woman and Nina, along with an ACS community specialist, set out to establish a teen board for the local American Cancer Society. The board's goal was "to organize and unify youth engagement by giving youth opportunity to make a meaningful contribution in the fight against cancer through education, advocacy, fundraising, and service." Together, they wrote up a mission statement, bylaws, and goals. The resolution passed at an ACS board meeting, and the first teen chapter in Wood County, West Virginia, was established.

The ACS Teens Board quickly mobilized the region's students, and they found themselves eager to reach out to their peers across the state and nation. When Nina discovered, to her surprise, that there was no such official organized effort for young volunteers nationwide, she determined to establish one. She proposed the idea to the ACS's CEO, and with his support, she worked with staff at the ACS national office to create this network.[4]

ACS Teens created innovative changes by restructuring the older model of youth volunteerism to fit today's teenagers and modern definitions of civic duty and activism. The program focused on creating a network of youth efforts, which was done through multiple communication tools—a Web site, newsletter, and conference calls. Youth were connected with their local ACS offices and given the opportunity to join together as leaders. They started school and community ACS Teens clubs that executed activities in education, public policy and advocacy, patient services, and fund-raising, at levels ranging from local to international. In just over one year, ACS Teens had young people representing all fifty states. ACS Teens then initiated Colleges Against Cancer, a service organization that now exists on over seventy campuses around the country.

But Nina didn't stop there. After being named the first youth member of the Nationwide Business Group of Voluntarism, she advocated for an in-depth focus on youth engagement. Thus, the National Youth Volunteer Involvement Task Force was convened, and Nina served as co-chairperson, helping put into place an official set of published best practices on youth empowerment, now used nationwide. One of the biggest changes that bringing youth to the forefront of ACS's agenda has made is in expanding the institutional culture. There is now official wording in ACS division charters that mandates a focus on youth volunteers. The ACS CEO recognized Nina for her "creative, groundbreaking work to involve teenagers in the ACS mission to eliminate cancer as a major health problem."

In our most recent interview with Nina in 2006, when she was twenty-two, she talked about the satisfaction she had received from pursuing her purpose. Achieving some of the goals she set out to accomplish in her cancer work has been the most rewarding part of her many activities, far outweighing the numerous honors and awards that she has received. One such accomplishment came when the West Virginia Senate passed a bill retargeting the corporate tobacco settlement funds to alleviate the state debt.

As Nina explained,

This bill not only would have left future West Virginians uneducated about the dangers of tobacco but also would have prevented those battling tobacco-related illnesses from proper access to treatment. I was alarmed that the existing political climate was preventing traditional advocacy groups from stepping forward, so I initiated a statewide public hearing on the bill and convinced fellow citizens to join me in speaking at the Capitol. I organized a petition and addressed the House of Delegates for ten minutes, explaining the importance of improving health and disease prevention while presenting an alternative solution to the debt crisis. A vote followed the hearing, and the bill was struck.

This bill would have had dangerous repercussions for my state, not only at the time but for over 20 years to come. I felt like I could actually see the impact that was made by successfully fighting the bill, it was such tangible change. In fact, this experience in activism was so positive that it fueled my dedication to politics and decision to major in Government in college. I have been fortunate enough to be a part of some incredible initiatives, but this one still stands out as the one that impacted my life the most, and means the most to me personally.

Not surprisingly, "grounded idealist" was first among the descriptors that Nina chose for herself. In fact, Nina has created a series of books for young adults, the "Saving the World" series, about leadership and social action, centered on the philosophy of "grounded idealism." The labels Nina chose for herself right after "grounded idealist" were "optimistic" and "self-confident," both of which indicate the markedly positive attitude to life that Nina shares with all the other highly motivated youth in our study.

A core element in a positive orientation is gratitude. Nina spoke for many of our purposeful youth when she told us: "I continue to be amazed by what the world has to offer." In our follow-up interview with her, she expressed her delight in discovering the many marvelous features of our world: "I'm starting to appreciate how special and wonderful it is just to *be*, and how lucky I am to be surrounded by people who exhibit so much love and beauty. I am so grateful and want to share this optimism and love for life with others. I guess that's how I find meaning." This sense of gratitude for being able to partake in what the world has to offer, and to have a chance to make one's own contribution, was common among all in our highly purposeful group.

What is so poignant about this, of course, is that this is the way that *all* young people should feel about life when they are starting out. Idealism, high hopes, enthusiasm, and a sense of awe and wonder in exploring the world around them are central to the traditional orientation of youth, noted by philosophers and writers since time immemorial. This is an attitudinal orientation that all young people deserve to have as their beginning stake in life. Yet this endowment of optimism and self-confidence seems restricted to only a portion of today's youth. In all of our society's current concerns about inequity, this one should top the list.

Nina's case also speaks to the power of an early discovery of purpose in leading the way to a satisfying adulthood. One emblematic hallmark of personal development, widely recognized since Erik Erikson placed it on our cultural radar screen a half century ago, is the forging of a personal identity. The great challenge during adolescence is to define oneself in a way that carves out a special place for the self in the world. A personal identity distinguishes the young person from all others, while at the same time it offers that person a model for becoming a valued member of society. A robust personal identity is the cornerstone of healthy psychological development later in adulthood.

In a study of self-understanding during adolescence, Daniel Hart and I found that one sure route to identity formation is to fashion a theory about the self based upon a systematic set of one's own values and beliefs.[5] Young people who see their own choices and destinies as part of something grander—whether it is a religious faith, a political ideology, a vocational calling, a lifestyle philosophy, or an aesthetic ideal—are well prepared to make the kind of mental commitment required to construct an enduring personal identity. Of course, not all young people build identities in this way; in fact, in our earlier study, only a few of the eighteen-year-olds, and none of the younger subjects, took this "systematic theory" route to identity formation.[6] For other youngsters, other successful routes are available. But those who said that they had adopted a strong belief system seemed to be unusually content and well directed.

In our present study, we noticed that several of the highly purposeful youth had fashioned their identities in this systematic, theoretically oriented way. Nina, for example, spoke with us at length about what she called her "combinatorial" view of how things work, and how this view inspires her to develop multiple sides of herself—scientist, policymaker, social entrepreneur, future physician, community and family member—in order to make her own best contribution:

> I am convinced that fighting serious illnesses that afflict our society requires a multilateral response. My cancer research involved a treatment that targeted many steps along the angiogenesis pathway to increase likelihood of therapeutic success. But this rationale extends beyond the drugs themselves to the broader ways in which we address and mitigate disease.

Medical progress comes from the "combination therapy" of simultaneously advancing not only scientific research, but also education, public health, business, and policy. Progress comes from solving problems using multiple perspectives. My childhood encounter with the laryngectomy patient demonstrated the importance of education in fostering wellness. Education is the first step, but for comprehensive change, we need to target multiple sectors of the healthcare system. I am motivated by this "combinatorial" framework, and consider it my leadership philosophy.

As this extraordinary testimony from Nina demonstrates, the pursuit of purpose fuels the development of a working theory that forms the basis of a systematic construction of self.

Several of the twelve young people in our study were keenly aware of the role of purpose in their search for personal identity. Pascal LeBoeuf, an aspiring musician, noted during one of our talks, "Well, I've found an identity. I've found something I enjoy doing. I have a love. That's pretty cool." In our conversations, Pascal elaborated an original and intricate theoretical viewpoint about his feelings toward music. "I want to create something for a certain reason," he told us. "I want to have some more direction behind it. It's deeper with something behind it. Art has a function . . . music has different functions, and I might do different types of music for different functions. . . . Instead of writing something and thinking, 'It makes me feel this way,' I try to think, 'How am I going to write something that makes me feel this way?' So, instead of the feeling coming from the art, I want the art to come from the feeling. And that makes me think about things like what technical or compositional elements can achieve a certain feeling. . . . So now I'm cursed because I won't be able to go back and randomly do that again. But I don't know, music without a purpose is kind of pointless."

As a young child, Pascal was fascinated by visual arts and spent hours at a time drawing with crayons. At nine, he was introduced to musical performance by a family friend who taught him to play "The Theme from the Pink Panther," "Greensleeves," and other tunes on the piano. "It was fun and interesting," Pascal recalls. Soon he was taking piano lessons ("My parents would always support my interests," he notes, "whether on not they liked them"). At age twelve, Pascal switched from classical to jazz. Throughout high school, he participated in jazz competitions, camps, and performance groups. By his last year in high school, Pascal's commitment to his music so dominated his time that he was taking only a few classes a day; yet he managed to do well enough in his academic program to consider applying to top colleges for a degree in engineering. But Pascal's musical interests prevailed, and he enrolled in the Manhattan School of Music for training in jazz composition and performance.

Pascal hopes to become a professional jazz musician. Of course jazz, like any performing art, is an extremely competitive field, and many young amateurs fail to make the transition to a career that can support their financial needs. Pascal is realistic about this: his propensity for theorizing about his musical aspirations does not mean that he has his head in the clouds about what it will take to achieve these aspirations. As noted above, this is another consistent characteristic of the purposeful youth we interviewed. They are practical. Pascal takes seriously the need to cultivate professional career goals, such as making contacts in the music industry and paying attention to the business side of things. As with his other thoughts on music, Pascal's thinking on accomplishing his financial, professional, personal, and musical goals is original and integrative: "I have to have them all within my life, and I want them all to be going on all the time. They're all goals that I want to happen. They all tend to depend on each other. My music is dependent on my friends. My creativity is dependent on what's going on in my life, how I'm experiencing things. My family is dependent on the business. The business is dependent on the creativity and the art." This holistic perspective spurs Pascal to devote his full energies to all aspects of his music career. He doesn't separate them into different compartments and value some aspects less. Such an approach is intrinsic to the extraordinary effectiveness of highly purposeful youth at an early age.

Barbara Brown, a girl from Texas who was sixteen years old when we first interviewed her, had learned the lesson of practical effectiveness through her work for environmental causes: "So I guess the completion of activities, really, would be a big obedience thing— or just listening and paying attention. So that has a big part in environmental work too, because if you don't get it right, it doesn't work. You've got to get it right. Especially when we apply for things . . . you really have to follow every little detail for it to be at all successful."

With two friends, Barbara played a key role in founding "Don't Be Crude," an organization that aims to improve the farmland environment by advocating for the proper disposal of motor fluids. She took on this cause after speaking with a friend who had noticed her father dumping used oil on his property, a practice that was common in rural areas in Texas where there were no other disposal facilities. "She noticed that her dad dumped oil on the ground and that it was killing the weeds," Barbara told us. "We needed something to do for 4-H that year in our club, so we decided to research it." Soon the girls were in touch with a state commission on environmental quality, which set them up to create a recycling program under the Elvis-reminiscent moniker "Don't Be Crude." The girls took to this challenge with zest. They started with one recycling container in their own county, but before long they had programs going in seven Texas counties protecting thousands of acres of groundwater along more than five hundred miles of coastline. In thinking about the meaning of her accomplishments, sixteen-year-old Barbara sounded much like our other highly purposeful youth in weaving together a theory about her relation to her cause:

> I guess [I'm interested in this] because I live out here, really. Everything that is out here is what we use. Our little pump out in the back. So I think that's a big part of it, just knowing that what I live off of, I take care of—and that, especially with what I do with oil recycling, it affects the groundwater which you pour it on. Whatever land you pour it on, if there's any water under it, it's going to get into it. And that's really a big part of it, that we live out here and we live off the water under our own land, then we're just polluting our own water systems. So I think that's why environmental is such a big deal, because I live out in the country, I live in the environment.

Note that the pattern of Barbara's discovery of her purpose is also similar to that of others in this group. She was introduced to the problem by someone outside her immediate family—in this case, a friend (although for others it has been teachers or other adults). There was a moment of revelation: something seemed wrong, needing correction or improvement. For Barbara, it was the sense that dumping used oil into the ground couldn't be doing the environment any good; for Ryan, it was the shock that some kids in Africa didn't have enough drinking water; for Nina, it was that people were dying of cancer unnecessarily; and for Pascal, it was that jazz music could be brought to new heights by his own creative passion.

In each case, the young person also found support from his or her immediate family and mentoring from people or organizations outside the family. In Barbara's case, a 4-H club played a crucial role by requiring that she do something for her community, and the Texas environmental commission introduced her to the specific possibility of running a recycling program. Once these young people got started, the initial successes they achieved added fuel to their motivation, and they became increasingly committed to their purpose, confident that they could do something about it, and eager to learn the skills they would need to do so.

Here is the sequence of steps we have identified in achieving a path of purpose:

1. Inspiring communication with persons outside the immediate family
2. Observation of purposeful people at work
3. First moment of revelation: something important in the world can be corrected or improved
4. Second moment of revelation: I can contribute something myself and make a difference
5. Identification of purpose, along with initial attempts to accomplish something
6. Support from immediate family

7. Expanded efforts to pursue one's purpose in original and consequential ways
8. Acquiring the skills needed for this pursuit
9. Increased practical effectiveness
10. Enhanced optimism and self-confidence
11. Long-term commitment to the purpose
12. Transfer of the skills and character strengths gained in pursuit of one purpose to other areas of life.

Once a young person has taken on a purposeful quest, his or her personality begins to be transformed by the activities and events of the quest. Out of necessity, the youngster acquires such capacities as resourcefulness, persistence, know-how, and a tolerance of risk and temporary setbacks. These capacities, of course, comprise many of the makings of a successful entrepreneur. Now, youngsters who fully commit themselves to challenging purposes likely are somewhat entrepreneurial in attitude to begin with, as their attraction to such missions shows. But it takes the experience of pursuing the quest to turn this entrepreneurial leaning into a full-blown entrepreneurial spirit, complete with the practical skills and dispositions required for mature social entrepreneurship.

Character virtues such as diligence, responsibility, confidence, and humility get a boost from the experience of making a commitment to a challenging purpose and seeing it through. What's more, literacies of all kinds (verbal, mathematical, cultural) develop in ways that extend well beyond anything previously learned in the youngster's home or classroom.

Perhaps most important, the young person's perspective on what is possible in the world (the potential as well as the limits of ambition) matures as a result of exposure to the inevitable mix of successes and failures that any entrepreneurial venture will produce. This can be enormously empowering for a young person's sense of confidence in his or her potential to make a difference in the world. It encourages young people to take on difficult tasks while at the same time preparing them for frustration (or even defeat) on some occasions. One of our subjects, who at age fifteen had fought and won a hard campaign for gun control legislation in his hometown, noted the realistic sense of empowerment that he acquired while working to advance his purpose:

> You can't sit there and govern your life based on what you're expecting will happen. You can't always be afraid to take a risk. You have to try different things, and maybe try things that you may think are a little extreme, maybe far-reaching, in terms of what you might accomplish. You think, "Oh, this is never going to happen. It's impossible, they'll never do that." Try it. Why not? . . . You just must get over the fear and say, no, it's not impossible. You really can do something and it doesn't require the multi-million-dollar funds that people spend on different issues. I think that people can really feel empowered that they can maybe do something.

The learning process takes time, requiring sustained commitment and hard work. But it is not an unpleasant process. In fact, from the report of our interviewees, the work is an enjoyable and emotionally satisfying process, reminiscent of the kinds of "flow" experiences that Mihaly Csikszentmihalyi describes. "Few things in life," Csikszentmihalyi has written, "are as enjoyable as when we concentrate on a difficult task, using all our skills, knowing what has to be done."[7] To their enduring benefit, highly purposeful youngsters learn this lesson early. A twenty-three-year-old high-tech aficionado, who creates complex computer programs and dynamic software, expressed his joy in the work this way:

> When I go home, some of my other friends can't understand that. They're like, "Uh, you work on computers all day. Why would you want to do that at home?" Yeah, but now I'm doing the fun stuff. Even at work it's the fun stuff. It's just so hard for a lot of people to understand. They just go home and think that I must be obsessed . . . I think that's why I like my work so much, just because it's challenging.

And, of course, the result of their work, when it accomplishes its mission, brings its own special kind of joy. Ryan told us: "When I went to Uganda for the first time to see the first well that was drilled; when I saw the people and how happy they were, just because they had clean water; here were these people dancing, celebrating, because they had clean water to drink. . . . It made me feel extremely good. So I was just very happy." All the others echoed Ryan's sentiments in their own ways.

The many personal benefits of pursuing purpose help explain why those young people who have found something to commit them-selves to tend to stick with it. They do not need external inducements once they get started. But they do need support—from family first and foremost, and from friends and others where available. Virtually all of our highly motivated youth, no matter how industrious or inventive they may have seemed, relied on crucial help from others at every phase of their engagement. They are determined, but not self-sufficient in any literal sense of the term—after all, they are still not completely educated or "raised" by the standards of our culture, despite their many accomplishments, and the tasks that they have committed themselves to are formidable by any standard.

Support for a young person's pursuit of purpose may come from many sources and in a wide variety of guises. In the cases of the twelve young people in our study, all had significant support from their parents—even though the parents did not introduce the particular purposes and often found them unfamiliar and perhaps a bit surprising. Nevertheless, the parents supported their children in the challenges they took on, often with invaluable assistance. Barbara Brown recalls:

> My dad is the brains of fixing things, especially when we started having problems with the units—he'd be like, "Okay!" And he'd call up the other dads, and he'd be, "Look, we've got this problem, let's work on it." . . . [And] once we got into grant writing, me and my mom would sit down and that's all we talk about. Just fill out these huge application forms.

Parents often also played an essential role in transporting and accompanying their children. When these children were too young to have their own driver's licenses, parents were needed as chauffeurs. At age twelve, Ryan was not old enough to do the extensive travel on his own that he was invited to do, so one of his parents always went with him on his trips and speaking engagements. Another parent, whose ten-year-old daughter was working to stop underage tobacco use, went so far as to accompany his child on undercover sting buys. The daughter would go into a local store to try to buy cigarettes (she was far beneath the legal age) while a concealed police officer watched. "We always called my dad the taxi driver because he would pick me up and take me here, all that," the girl told us. At the same time, her mother offered her constant emotional support. "My mom's a psychotherapist, so we talk about everything. We take family vacations, and it's a very close family."

Beyond parents, other adult mentors can play critical roles. Indeed, it is often an outside adult who introduces the purpose or encourages the young person to take up the cause. Nina Vasan points to the importance of her relationship with her adult mentor in her efforts to find a way to contribute to the fight against cancer. The woman encouraged Nina to create and lead a teen cancer organization; she helped Nina write the bylaws for the new organization; she showed Nina how to work with the American Cancer Society; and she instructed her in the intricacies of fund-raising. "She helped me prepare by anticipating questions potential donors and grant committees would ask, explained the importance of backing up proposals with data and evidence, and in general helped guide me through the nonprofit and political worlds." Nina sums up her experience this way: "She has been my mentor, and has helped me define who I am and understand what my role is in the world."

In some cases, highly purposeful youth look to multiple mentors for instruction, support, and inspiration. Pascal, for example, has studied under several music teachers over the years and considers all of them his mentors. He also has learned from "just random musicians in New York, people that I admire." Another of our subjects, twenty-three-year-old Michael Davidson, who (rare in this generation) has been active politically and is committed to political change, has found mentors in family members, a work supervisor, and one of his high school teachers. The teacher was one of Michael's strongest influences: "My senior year in high school, my high school government professor got me academically and intellectually interested in politics. . . . He was just impassioned about the subject. And he was rigorous, he gave us a lot to read, it was an AP course but I just loved it. I just ate it up." Another of Michael's mentors "believed in and supported me more than I did myself" and "was most responsible for encouraging me to emotionally commit to my newfound passion." When he died, "I gave the eulogy on how this guy, this man affected my life and he was like a father to me in a lot of ways. . . ." Another young person also gave credit to multiple mentors for her achievements: "I had great mentors beyond my parents. And this is why this work is ultimately so important, because of the mentors that I've had. And this goes to the community aspect, [because] there have been professionals who have taken a nonparental role with me."

Purposeful youth also draw support from their peers: like most adolescents and young adults, they value their friendships highly and respond to them in ways that cannot be replicated in relationships with adults. But these highly motivated youngsters usually find that old friends do not share their newfound passion. Their solution, then, is to actively seek out new friendships with peers who are working toward the same goals that have inspired them. Pascal spoke in the same vein as all the others when he told us, "It's easier now because all my friends are musicians at school. In high school, it wasn't like that. I had friends and then I had music. Now they're the same."

In a side project that closely examined the lives of all the highly purposeful people in our study, educational psychologist Kendall Cotton Bronk wrote: "These youth found a few friends among their school peers who shared their interests, but for the most part, their classmates were uninterested in the purposes that inspired them. However, these adolescents, going against the grain, remained dedicated to their aims and actively sought out communities of like-minded peers."[8]

Highly purposeful youth are so intensely focused on their missions that they sometimes build other decisions, such as whom to choose as friends, around those missions. But it would not be accurate to call them single-minded. Indeed, these youngsters have all the same interests as their peers. As we saw at the start of this chapter, they are fundamentally normal adolescents. They care about a host of things, including many that are frivolous. They are certainly noteworthy in their dedication, their achievements, and in all the capacities and skills they have learned in the course of their efforts. They also have managed to avoid, through stable commitments, the debilitating sense of drift that is plaguing so many others in their generation; and they pursue their commitment with a zest for risk and challenge, and a resourcefulness, that is characteristic of budding entrepreneurs. All these extraordinary fruits of purpose, with their salutary benefits and byproducts, stem from the same genotype as that shared by every other youngster on the planet.

It is the combination of normalcy and exceptional initiative that makes this group so informative to us. Their experiences offer lessons that are wholly relevant to all young people growing up today. I am reminded of the somewhat odd but well-received computer-animated movie *Ratatouille*, which I saw recently. It tells the story of a cute and talented rat who wants to become a master chef, and the message of his success is: "Anyone can cook!" Just so—our study results convince me that *anyone can find purpose and pursue it with rich benefit to themselves and others.* But, as I have pointed out, support is vital along the way.

5

Beyond a Culture of Short Horizons

The single greatest barrier to youngsters finding their paths to purpose is the fixation on short horizons that infuses cultural messages sent to young people today. A popular culture celebrating quick results and showy achievements has displaced the traditional values of reflection and contemplation that once stood as the moral north star of human development and education. Instant mass communication transmits tales of highly envied people who have taken shortcuts to fame and fortune to every child with access to computers and televisions (and that amounts to just about every child in any industrial society). Among the most common formats for television shows at present are contests in which ordinary young people rocket to fame and fortune in a matter of minutes, days, or, at most, weeks. The appeal of quick material success is amplified by current economic conditions, which have led to unparalleled abundance and affluence for some, fierce global competitiveness for others, and the specter of deprivation for many others.

Out of a mixture of status-seeking, acquisitiveness, insecurity, self-promotion, and just plain superficial values, the agents of today's culture are urging young people to pursue short-term victories at the expense of enduring aspirations. The sad irony is that, for many of today's young, the short-term goals are not holding up—they cannot hold up—long enough to achieve even the desired material ends. The quick routes to fortune and happiness showcased by mass media are little more than Hollywood-type fantasies. Any success in life, from the mundane to the spiritual, requires sustained effort. The more lasting and fulfilling kinds of success require a deeper reflection on the purposes that underlie the efforts. Developmentally, the proper period in life to begin such reflection is during adolescence, when a youngster begins to make choices about what kind of person to become and what kind of life to lead.

Youth is a time of idealism—or at least it should be. There is ample time later to rein in one's dreams to conform to the inevitable constraints of the world; but a human life that does not begin with idealistic aspirations is likely to be a barren one. Philosophers, psychologists, and other close observers of human development have agreed on this for centuries. Aristotle put it this way over two thousand years ago: "They are hopeful, their lives are filled with expectation, they are high-minded, they choose to do what is noble rather than what is expedient—such, then, is the character of the young."

In today's nervously competitive world, youthful idealism is giving way to a single-minded desire for material gain and financial security. Researchers surveying student beliefs and goals in the early college years have concluded:

Especially notable are changes in the importance given to two contrasting values: "developing a meaningful philosophy of life" and "being very well off financially." In the late 1960s, developing a meaningful philosophy of life was the top value, endorsed as an "essential" or "very important" goal by more than 80% of the entering freshmen. "Being very well-off financially," on the other hand, lagged far behind, ranking fifth or sixth on the list with less than 45% of the freshmen endorsing it as a very important or essential goal in life. Since that time, these two values have basically traded places, with being very well-off financially now the top value (at 74.1% endorsement) and developing a meaningful philosophy of life now occupying sixth place at only 42.1% endorsement.[1]

This shift did not take place in a vacuum. Our popular media emphasize the allure of material success, especially of the quick-hit kind. What's more, with best intentions, adults in recent years have been busy talking young people out of their natural idealism and into a posture of heightened material concern. Often this is done out of a sense of fearful expedience, for the sake of helping the young person get ahead in today's competitive marketplace. Such a stance is shaky for young people not only because it is unnatural for their period of life but also because it has no sustaining conviction of its own. It is a timid and pessimistic stance that inspires neither wholehearted effort nor lasting allegiance.

My intention is not to disparage material pursuits during youth or other periods of life. All people need, and enjoy, certain material possessions. As for money, it is beyond doubt key to achieving many of life's goals. A large part of helping children learn how to pursue their dreams in a realistic way entails teaching them how to manage the financial demands of their chosen paths. But children must understand that money is a means to an end—hopefully, a noble one—rather than an end in itself. It is the glamorization of money for its own sake, as little more than a superficial ego boost, that leads young people down barren paths. The "quick hit" mentality that I have referred to only bolsters this fruitless orientation. By suggesting that success can be achieved without hard work and years of preparation, it implies that the things that can be quickly acquired if one is lucky—such as fame and material fortune—are themselves sufficient for true success. The reason I object to this suggestion is that true success requires a sense of meaning that runs deeper than fortune or fame. The accumulation of material success without an ultimate concern, some larger purpose that the material success is meant to serve, is a prescription for a dispiriting sense of emptiness once the initial glow of self-gratification has worn off.

The predominant cultural messages today are convincing many young people to exert energetic (sometimes frantic) efforts in pursuit of achievement, but they have failed to help them find deeper purpose in the efforts they are making. The messages press for ratcheted-up achievement unconnected to ultimate concerns, higher performances that have little personal meaning for the child. What's more, in too many of our conversations with our young, we fail to discuss the fundamental questions with them, as if this would slow them down in their race to get ahead. In our headlong rush—and theirs—we are not only losing sense of what's worthwhile to strive for, we are also depleting a main source of enduring motivation for a young person.

Goals for the short term—finishing a homework assignment,

getting good grades, making the team, finding a date for the prom—come and go from day to day. They may be necessary for adapting to a present situation; and young people can learn important skills while pursuing these short-term goals. But they cannot, in themselves, define an agenda for the future. Short-horizon thinking cannot help a young person define a desired self-identity (What kind of person do I wish to become?) nor can it produce an inspiring purpose to dedicate oneself to (What do I want to accomplish with my life?). It can serve to get through the moment—sometimes necessary, to be sure—but not to create the kinds of forward momentum that lead to lasting satisfaction.

Our cultural focus on short horizons no doubt stems from—or at least is accelerated by—insecurities that we face in our increasingly fast-paced global economy. We worry about the competition that we and our children are up against in seeking to provide the basic necessities of shelter, education, health. How can we allow ourselves to get distracted by big-picture matters (and the *Why* question is the biggest-picture matter of all) when someone may be trying to eat our lunch right in front of us? Ironically, though, our efforts to be protectively pragmatic for the sake of our young have left them *less* equipped to deal with the complexities of today's world. A short-term approach born of anxiety cannot foster the imagination and nerve needed to thrive in a highly dynamic contemporary society. Only a long view, fueled by energetic purposes, can build and sustain the capacities that will be needed.

In place of asking the ultimate questions, we have been directing the attention of our young toward short-term concerns of competition, self-promotion, status, and material gain. We may believe that attention to such concerns is in their best interests; but in the end we will always find that single-minded attention to such concerns can promote nothing more than ambivalence, disengagement, and cynicism. Still, rather than encouraging our young to pursue the interests that motivate and inspire them, we try to substitute our own concerns and goals for them. We turn a deaf ear to their pursuit of meaning—their own attempt to answer the big questions—and try to bring them back to our fearful concerns. It is a futile attempt.

BEYOND SHORT-HORIZON THINKING IN OUR SCHOOLS

Laudably, our society has become increasingly serious about education during the past few decades. Every U.S. politician now has a position supporting school improvement, and business leaders have weighed in on the importance of an educated population for competitiveness in the global marketplace. Philanthropists are dedicating vast resources to efforts aimed at ensuring that every schoolchild gains the competence needed for work and citizenship. As with any serious effort, approaches vary according to the politics and worldviews of those making the effort. But with few exceptions, all of the major approaches to school improvement today have one thing in common: they measure progress almost entirely by the standardized test scores of students.

I am not one of the many critics of tests, grades, and other objective measures of student achievement. I favor explicit standards of achievement and believe that competition, when kept in perspective, benefits student learning. But the standardized tests that schools in the United States use today have little to do with advancing standards of excellence in learning, understanding, or gaining useful knowledge. Instead, the tests that we rely on to determine whether a student is learning (and whether a school is doing its job well) are used to provide evidence for those who wish to evaluate the student or the school system. The tests are intended to have "high stakes" for student and school. As such, the tests draw attention away from other educational priorities, in particular the core missions of encouraging the acquisition of active knowledge and a lifelong love of learning. Often squeezed entirely out of the school day are questions of meaning and purpose that should underlie every academic exercise. In place of these broader goals, the main objective of the classroom becomes imparting a rapid familiarity with facts, names, places, and formulas that students have little interest or skill in applying to problems beyond the classroom.

Critics have complained, rightly I believe, that our obsessive reliance on standardized test scores deters both teachers and students from concentrating on the real mission of schooling: developing a love of learning for learning's sake—a love that will then lead to self-maintained learning throughout the lifespan. I agree with this frequently voiced opinion, with the caveat that test taking does not in itself diminish anything else, including love of learning. But if test taking becomes the sole, or even primary, concern of those who establish a school's agenda—and here I include everyone from those who pay the bills to those who teach the classes—the most important items on the agenda tend to get squeezed out. Among those items, as the critics have noted, is deep learning.

Every bit as important, though not often noticed, is a student's quest for meaning in the demands and activities of the school day. It is essential to ask—and young people always do—what, if any, is the relation between what a student does at school and any larger purpose that could attract his or her interests, energies, and eventual commitment. This is the *Why* question that I have raised throughout this book, directed this time at the classrooms and assignments that occupy much of a young person's waking time.

As I commented at the outset of this book, it is rare to hear a teacher discuss with students the broader purpose that any of their academic activities might lead to, or even make any mention of the satisfaction, interest, or enjoyment that many people find in such pursuits. Why do mathematicians labor over the proofs that students must learn, and why do scientists conduct the experiments that fill the textbooks? Why do we read literature or go to watch a Shakespeare play? The answers to these questions may seem obvious to us as adults; but children have no way of knowing about the appeal of such activities unless they either experience them themselves or have a chance to observe others who have been moved by their own experience. When students get that chance, it can make a powerful impression on them. Teachers can engage even the most inattentive, raucous students by expressing their own appreciation for subjects that they themselves have been genuinely interested in. I have seen a tough inner-city classroom begin to pay attention after the teacher talked passionately about how much a great work of literature moved her when she was young—the students dropped their usual facades of cool bravado and listened intently, taking it in with open-eyed wonder.

But all too often the most fundamental and intriguing questions that could awaken students' interest in learning go unasked and unanswered—even those that teachers know about personally. *Why would someone study the craft of teaching and seek a job as a teacher?* Teachers rarely discuss with students the reasons that motivated them to go into the profession. Nor do they often offer inspiring comments about the satisfactions they have experienced in their calling. What kind of an example is this for students just beginning to think about the meaning of a vocation? How can we expect that a student will find an enduring sense of purpose if we are constantly drawing the student's attention away from considerations of long-term aspiration and personal meaning?

If we never provide students with information about what adults they admire find meaningful; if we never tell them about how those adults searched for purpose; if we never give them occasions for reflecting on their own searches and encourage them to ask the essential questions about what they want to do with their lives, we risk raising a generation that enters adulthood without direction—or, worse yet, hesitates to enter adulthood at all.

Young people take advice about seeking fulfillment seriously. In the world of pressures, competition, job requirements, and other responsibilities that they hear about endlessly, how can they manage to find something that is both realistic and meaningful? Teachers rarely address this crucial question. But it is the question that, sooner or later, all young people must confront in order to make the choices that will shape their lives.

Our schools—at least the better ones—are adept at building basic skills; and our colleges and universities expose young people to a rich array of ideas and knowledge. All such educational gifts can enrich a student's intellectual life in immeasurable ways. But when it comes to guiding students toward paths that they will find personally rewarding and meaningful, so many of today's schools and colleges fall short. In the lessons that they offer students, most schools and colleges emphasize specialized knowledge that students have limited use for.

From time to time, almost in passing (as during those fleeting moments of school commencements), distinguished leaders urge students to go out and do great things in the world. But when it comes to drawing a connection between their specialized academic lessons and these larger aspirations—that is, showing how mathematical or historical knowledge might contribute to a larger purpose a student wishes to pursue—students are pretty much left on their own. Such connections are not part of the curriculum and certainly not part of a teacher's or professor's job description.

Perhaps this kind of advice should be the role of guidance or career counselors. If so, our schools and colleges have not seen fit to support such a role. The ratio of guidance counselors to students in most U.S. schools at present is far too low; and finding career-counseling services in many colleges takes you on a journey into the furthest reaches of the academic backwater. Making a connection between what students are learning academically and how they can find careers that will be meaningful to them is one of the lowest priorities at our contemporary academic institutions, well behind football, celebrity appearances, and new dining halls.[2]

In our secondary schools and colleges alike, few instructors spend time discussing with students the wider meaning of what they are doing day to day—an odd omission for institutions dedicated to intellectual examination and critical questioning. This "meaning gap" extends from the student's present activities to his or her future prospects: in both cases, students too often are mystified about the relevance of their schoolwork to the knowledge skills that they will need to use. In a broader sense, it is even less likely that classroom instruction will lead students to reflect on such essential questions as "what kind of person do I want to become?" Or "what is the meaning of my life?" Such questions seem too airy for many educators, even in philosophy courses. Yet they are central to becoming a fully educated person.

BEYOND THE CULTURE OF SHORT HORIZONS IN THE COMMUNITY AND THE MEDIA

What about other places where young people spend their time—in our communities and absorbing the popular culture? What kinds of guidance do our young encounter here? This is the greatest lottery in youth development. Some young people are fortunate to have adult mentors who introduce them to goals and purposes that inspire them, and also to practical means of achieving these goals and purposes. Some will benefit from high-quality presentations of the arts, history, and literature that our media and educational institutions, at their best, are capable of producing.

But many of today's young will drift along, from lack of opportunity or encouragement, with no such exposure. They will be at the mercy of media influences that showcase the most salacious, frivolous, and materialistic elements of our society. Any random tour through the Web sites, cable TV shows, popular books, and music marketed to the young would produce enough examples of this degraded mix to fill a warehouse. One description of the way our contemporary mass media markets to young people is "the race to the bottom."[3]

The recent surge of interest in purpose throughout the culture is itself revealing. As we noted at the beginning of chapter 2, the ancient *idea* of the need for purpose has been gathering steam in science and in literature.[4] But purpose *in practice* is in too short supply in our society, especially with respect to the way we raise and educate our young. Could it be that today's writers are paying attention to this essential component of human thriving because they recognize, whether consciously or not, that it now may be endangered by the way we organize our family and societal affairs?

My intent here is not to serve as a voice against contemporary cultural decline—there are more than enough media critics these days happy to fill that role—but rather to point out that the acculturation of young people does not happen by itself. Adults must be active in creating a wholesome cultural environment that sets standards in both a constraining and an inspiring sense. From the cultural information that they receive, young people learn *boundaries*—what's permissible to do and what's not—and also *positive examples*—what it is possible to aim for in one's search for achievement and fulfillment. This is the social learning that the adult community must provide for its young people if they are to find a positive direction in life. If we leave the source of such social learning to chance, some youngsters will find productive paths on their own; many others will become confused or misled by the culture's many corrosive influences.

Consider, for example, a young person looking for advice about what kind of career path to follow. Secondary schools, as we have seen, are woefully unprepared to offer such advice, and it is rare to find a college that invests much in this effort. Some parents or relatives may offer some helpful tips, but most are either not sufficiently informed about the current world of work or they have their own biases ("You should go into my business") that may discredit them in the eyes of young listeners. So, young people are left with what they observe through the eyes of the mass media. Hollywood presents them with glamorized, two-dimensional portraits of workers that reveal none of the real-world concerns about the actual challenges, opportunities, and rewards of various fields. As for books, in 2006 two of the top best-sellers among personal finance books unabashedly transmitted the message that the only careers worth aspiring to are those that bring great wealth. One of these contrasted a successful entrepreneur with a teacher, who was described as ending up a "broken man."[5] Another baldly asserted that "middle class people are mediocre in their field, and poor people are poor in their field."[6] Even the *Wall Street Journal*, no enemy of plutocrats, complained in a review of this book: "Police officers and nuns everywhere might reasonably take offense at that kind of sentiment."[7] But few young people have the experience or maturity of judgment of a seasoned book reviewer. As they consume these and similar cultural messages, they can only conclude that most of the career paths available to them—many of which are essential for society and deeply fulfilling for those who pursue them—are only for losers.

None of this is helpful for someone at the crossroads of emerging adulthood. In fact, it is worse than unhelpful: it is factually wrong, misleading, and discouraging. What would be helpful is an approach that guides a young person's attention away from short-term, extraneous goals that bring little lasting satisfaction—the noise in the atmosphere—and toward pursuits that will bring personal meaning now and in the future. In a broader sense, young people also need to hear cultural messages that inspire them to participate as active citizens in our society. Largely because of what they see in media accounts of public officials, as I noted earlier, too many young people have turned away from civic and political interests.

Neither our media outlets nor our public leaders pay enough attention these days to young people's attitudes about civic life. Encouraging a positive affiliation with the civic society is not a high priority for schools, media, or any other agents of our popular culture. This can only be because we have lost sight of what matters for the long term in a person's development. We must recapture that longer and more enlightened view. As a revered international leader of an earlier era, Dag Hammarskjöld, once said, "Only he who keeps his eyes fixed on the far horizon will find the right road." It is our responsibility as adults in this uncertain, confusing, and increasingly cynical time to provide the younger generation with far-horizon guidance.

BEYOND SHORT-HORIZON GUIDANCE
IN OUR HOMES

Recently, a parent sent me the following e-mail:

A couple of months ago, my daughter turned to me one morning and said that she had watched a documentary on human trafficking and how young girls were being sold into slavery and she was horrified that such a thing could occur, that she heard it was occurring in many countries, even in America, and that she just had to do something about it. I said, why didn't she start an awareness program at school, maybe raise money for efforts to combat the problem? I said this would be a great idea because she could write it up and put it on her college application and it would look great to prospective colleges. At which point she turned to me and said, with some disappointment, not to mention cynicism,

"That's right, Mom, it's all about me, isn't it?" I was suitably abashed at the time, and then saw in a very concrete way how I was contributing to the problem that you were discussing. It's a small example, but it's one that shows how often, in an attempt to make our children competitive in the marketplace, we take any concern they may have for the welfare of others, something that might become a long-term purpose, and we turn it into a short-term, self-serving goal.

I quote this e-mail here not because it is startling or unusual but, to the contrary, because it is an example of adult-child interchanges that I have witnessed frequently over the past few years.

Young people are more astute than adults around them may realize. They see through to the core of guidance that is motivated by little more than calculated self-promotion or, yet more discouragingly, abject self-protectiveness. They are aware of the cynicism at its center. Out of respect for those who utter such advice, they may see fit to get with the program, but rarely with enthusiasm.

Oddly, the pressures toward bald expedience that many young people encounter usually have little to do with genuine material need. Indeed, the strongest pressures often come from the most affluent families. David is a recent college graduate who spent some summers with a charitable group dedicated to serving indigent children. After college, he intended to work full time with the group, helping them organize their fund-raising efforts and doing administrative work for them. The pay would have been subsistence-level, and David did not know where it would lead—perhaps to a career in philanthropy or medicine, or perhaps to a management or business career with a focus on social enterprise, or to a public service legal career. It would have been hard and uncertain work, but David's eyes shone when he spoke of it. His father, however, was vigorously opposed, saying that David should earn an advanced degree before taking on such work. A wealthy, self-made businessman, David's father likely saw the world as a viciously competitive place that was becoming even more that way all the time. Perhaps the father feared that David would fall behind and never catch up if he spent years of his youth on an ill-defined charitable mission.

The confrontation between father and son escalated to the extent that they each voiced relationship-breaking threats—shutdown communication, disinheritance, curses—in the heat of many moments. Finally, the two backed away from the brink, but not before lasting mistrust and hard feelings had developed between them. Ultimately, David took a year off and did some part-time volunteer work for the group while applying to law school programs. His applications have not yet been successful: perhaps they reflect his lack of enthusiasm for this course. In any event, David still faces an uncertain future, although now with markedly less confidence, passion, or commitment.

First efforts in life are important because they can be formative in development.[8] We can safely predict that before David will be able to move on with confidence to a satisfying career, he will need to come to terms with the conflicts that attended his initial attempts at making a serious contribution. In the worst cases, a snowball of negative associations starts rolling and keeps growing throughout life as it gathers size and momentum. A deferred dream becomes interpreted as a personal failure, which then is interpreted as a statement about the inadequacy of self, which then becomes interpreted as a reason to defer or decline other dreams, and so on down the cycle of hopelessness and self-defeat. This is why it is so important to support a young person's early efforts. It is essential to encourage the kinds of efforts that will lead the young person in productive and fulfilling directions in the long run.

For many of today's young, a first effort with long-standing (though surprisingly little noticed) consequence is the college application. The college application is often the first serious chance that students have to present their plans, goals, and accomplishments to highly respected places that will evaluate and either accept or reject them. The way that students approach this task sets the tone for other acts of self-presentation to come. Will they feel confident as they present themselves for further evaluation throughout their lives? Will they learn to put their best foot forward truthfully when representing prior accomplishments, or will they exaggerate, distort, and make things up?

The questions that arise directly for the college application are: Will students openly state what they are looking for in a college education, or will they just try to figure out what the college wants to hear from them? And most directly to the point, will they even write their own applications?

It would be naive to ignore the barely hidden secret that many college applications these days are largely the product of a parent's pen; and that the presentations of self embedded in students' statements of intent are often disingenuous at best and dishonest at worst. I have consulted with admissions departments at prominent colleges in recent years, and I can recite almost from memory the scripts that students and their parental editors write in efforts to get on the good side of admissions officials: *I intend to make a difference in the world; take on many challenges; aim high; follow my passions; learn all that there is to know about my field of choice; contribute to my community in college and beyond; and devote myself to improving the human condition.* All of which can be wonderfully self-fulfilling sentiments when they emanate sincerely from the student. In some cases, certainly, they do. But for many students, using these kinds of statements to fill in lines of a college application is little more than an empty exercise in posing and fabricating, under the watchful eye of a parent who manages the act and writes much of the script.

What's wrong with this? On the plus side, it certainly demonstrates the parent's concern and affection for the child. In addition, any help from a parent affords the child a chance to learn valuable practical skills from the parent's greater experience. And doesn't every student have the right to compete for the best opportunities available? Why shouldn't a parent do whatever it takes to get a child into the most prestigious college possible? There are many good reasons to provide guidance and help for a child in any situation, including application to college.

Yet any approach that substitutes an adult's efforts for a child's, rather than supporting the child's own efforts, has a number of unintended consequences. In a moral sense, it is less than honest; and participating intentionally in a dishonest act with a child can send the child the wrong message about truth.[9] In a practical sense, finding the right match in a college is far more important for a student's ultimate happiness than securing a spot in the most prestigious place. It is counterproductive to shade the truth about the child's true accomplishments, goals, and interests, because the prevarication stands in the way of finding the right match. Many students, driven by their status-seeking parents, squeeze into places they don't belong, only to discover after some failure that their interests and potentials are better recognized and fulfilled elsewhere. They may then need to disrupt their studies to seek another course; and the lost time and attendant risks are unnecessary. These concerns are well known by educators everywhere.

DEEPENING THE WELL OF PARENTAL GUIDANCE

In a change that is largely for the good, today's young are communicating with parents and other adults more intensely and more earnestly than have the young people of previous recent cohorts. It is common now to hear baby boomer parents note, with a mix of bemusement and delight, that their kids talk to them frequently and at length about their most intimate and serious problems, actually *asking their parents* for advice. "The last people in the world I would have gone to about a decision would have been my folks," many adults of my age say. "But my kids, amazingly, seem to want my opinion!"

As with any social change, all kinds of explanations are tossed around to account for this. One businessman friend of mine suggested that it is simply a function of cell phones and cheaper long-distance phone rates. A sociological study has found that, in general, people today are close to their families but isolated from neighbors, meaning that we are increasingly likely to discuss important matters only with core family members such as Mom and Dad. According to this study, "the general image is one of a densely connected, close, homogenous set of ties slowly closing in on itself, becoming smaller, more tightly interconnected, more focused on the very strong bonds of the nuclear family (spouses, parents, and partners)."[10] This provides welcome benefits of more intimate and more frequent parent-child communication.

Such communication offers parents expanded opportunities to influence their children in powerful ways. But we do not always take good advantage of these opportunities. Parents may not know how to use their intimate discussions with children to offer guidance that the children can find constructive and meaningful. Consequently, the guidance that young people receive about the ultimate questions in their lives—goals they might wish to accomplish, future directions they would find meaningful, causes worth striving for, and their very reasons for being—is too often empty of larger purpose. In such cases, as with the girl quoted in the parent's e-mail above, young people may find the advice uncomfortably self-serving and uninspiring, and they may come away with feelings of dejection and stress rather than a sense of encouragement or hope.

Young people treasure guidance from experienced adults who care about them and know more about the world than they do. To be most helpful—and welcome—the guidance must speak to the youngster's highest aspirations. But it does not need to humor unrealistically romantic dreams about mastering the universe. Young people do not wish to be shielded from hard realities; they wish to learn how to accomplish their dreams in the face of such realities. Informing them of the actual steps they must take in order to achieve their highest aspirations is educative in the best sense of the word.

The problem is that many young people are not receiving guidance that respects their deepest purposes while at the same time providing them with constructive practical advice. Too often what they hear from the important adults in their lives are dire warnings and crafty strategies for beating the competition. When this happens, young people are not learning realistic ways to pursue their purposes; rather, they are learning that the purposes themselves are unrealistic, without being shown any alternative that could inspire them. We can do better than this. In our homes and throughout our communities, we can help children much more effectively pursue their highest aspirations in a realistic manner. The next chapter offers specific guidance to parents, and all adults in children's lives, about how to foster the discovery of a sense of purpose.

6

Parenting for Purpose

"Are some kids born purposeful, or is this something that everyone needs to learn?" "What can parents do to help their children gain a sense of purpose?" "How can I talk to my child about purpose without seeming preachy or intrusive?"

These are some "FAQs" that I hear when I speak to parent groups about my research on youth purpose. I certainly don't pretend to have all the answers to raising children these days. In fact, I tend to describe myself as a "survivor" of three adolescents, and in the midst of the many joys of parenthood I have often felt totally bewildered. But I do believe that the findings I've discussed in this book offer important guidelines for parents on the all-important matter of fostering a sense of purpose in their children. The difficulties of some of the young people quoted in chapters 1 and 3, and the lessons of the highly purposeful profiled in chapter 4, reveal several vital conclusions.

My intention here is not to offer a general guide to parenting, but rather to highlight a number of specific ways in which parents can be most effective in this particular mission of fostering purpose. The approach that I describe is a highly engaged one, hinging on parents' regularly sharing their values and outlooks on life with their children, and also listening carefully for expressions of interest and acting in a range of ways to support that interest. A good deal has been written of late about "helicopter parenting," but, as I commented earlier, this and similar criticism of parental involvement miss a key point. Parents *should* be attentive to and engaged in their children's lives. The key is that they not become domineering.

Parenting has been buffeted by many fluctuating trends. After a time, old practices seem not only out of date but even foolish. The Progressive Era of the early twentieth century, supported by the emerging science of psychology, ushered in a new concern for children's thoughts and feelings whereby traditional Victorian sensibility that children were "best seen but not heard" was transformed into a doctrine of "child-centeredness." This doctrine came to dominate child-rearing practices for the rest of the century to the point that parents were advised, in the words of one influential author, to always "put children first": to listen carefully to their desires, to respect their ideas, to relieve them of frustrating experiences, and to boost their self-esteem whenever possible.[1] This kinder and gentler approach was considered an unquestionable step forward from the insensitive harshness of prior practice.

Yet by the end of the twentieth century, a reaction had set in against what was by then seen as the overindulgence of excessively child-centered and permissive parenting. Newspapers ran stories about skyrocketing rates of youth criminality, and perturbed adults exchanged stories about the unruly and ill-mannered behavior of children next door, or worse, on crowded planes and in public places. Books with such titles as *Because I Said So, Spoiled Rotten, No,* and my own *Greater Expectations* began to appear on the parenting shelves, and the once-antiquated notions of discipline, parental authority, and behavioral standards regained their appeal.

Such changes in social trends can be healthy to the extent that they are driven by adaptations to new circumstances or by corrections in courses that have been shown to be misguided. The child-centered revolution of the early twentieth century led to many improvements in the way we treat children, ranging from the abolition of child labor to the improved communication between parents and children today. In the same spirit, the contemporary "Say Yes to No" movement (which some parents have even organized around)[2] can be seen as an effort to correct for the problem of children developing the notion that whatever they are doing, no matter how disruptive or inept, is automatically praiseworthy.

We must always be wary, though, that as new trends set in, they create their own distortions and blind spots, which must themselves be guarded against and swiftly counteracted. Too often, we fail for a long time to recognize the unfortunate by-products of new trends. It took much too long for our society to realize that the Progressives' beneficial concern for children's psychological security and well-being had morphed into a weakening of basic rules and standards for children; and the casualties of that delay are still making headlines. Now, stronger parental guidance has come back into fashion. But this change, inevitably, will be accompanied by new risks. We must continually examine our most accepted assumptions about what young people need, in order to avoid falling lockstep into any trend that, no matter how sensible it may appear, will always have its own short-comings.

Whatever I or anyone else has written about the merits of discipline, one thing is plain: "no" cannot serve as a sufficient guide to parenting. And as for standards, as I noted in chapter 1 of this book, it is a mistake to think that young people can thrive over the long haul unless they find personal meaning in whatever standards they attempt to achieve.

These cautions about any given set of specific guidelines for parenting having been stated, I am entirely confident in asserting that the urgent project for parents today, in this world of increasing economic, cultural, and social uncertainty, is to help their children gain a wholesome sense of direction that will carry them through the minefields of drift, confusion, apathy, anxiety, fear, and self-absorption that threaten their generation. I am also convinced that the key to this sense of direction is finding a life purpose. While a parent cannot simply give a purpose to a child, and indeed any too forceful or controlling effort to do so is likely to have adverse repercussions, nonetheless there is much that the parent can do.

All parents have rich life experience and a certain degree of acquired wisdom; and there is no question that children benefit from being exposed to these parental gifts. The key is the way in which a parent seeks to guide the child toward a purpose that is genuine to the child's own self. Parents must not be too commanding or overly assertive. As many have discovered, children don't generally take well to being lectured to, or commanded, especially in an area as deeply personal as finding a sense of genuine purpose. Children must have a sense that they are finding their way toward purposes of their own choosing, and parents cannot make these choices for them.

What a parent *should* do is lead a child toward promising options. A parent can help a child sort through choices and reflect upon how the child's talents and interests match up with the world's opportunities and needs. A parent can support a child's own efforts to explore purposeful directions, and open up more potential sources of discovery about possible purposes. These are supporting roles rather than leading ones, because center stage in this drama belongs to the child. But while the most effective assistance parents can provide is indirect, it is also invaluable.

I can hear some parents asking themselves, But how much can I really do?

ARE SOME KIDS BORN MORE PURPOSEFUL THAN OTHERS?

In recent years, developmental science has discovered an increasing number of natural capacities and dispositions that children bring with them into this world. From studies of newborn and infant behavior, we know that all healthy children are capable of empathy, attachment to their caregivers, language learning, and a host of other pro-social acts. We also know that there are individual differences among children at birth, and that some of these differences have consequences for the kinds of personalities they will develop. Some children are more active than others; some are shy, others gregarious; and some are born with exceptional physical motor skills that give them the advantage on an athletic field or in a concert hall. As we learn more from studies of brain, behavior, and genetic dispositions, we shall surely find more natural tendencies that we can ascribe to biological inheritance.

Yet I am certain that we shall never discover a gene for purpose. In order to find purpose, children must survey the world around them and determine where and how they can make their own contribution. They must get to know themselves well enough to see how their own talents and interests match some niche that the world has to offer. This means that they must come to understand both themselves and the world that they are growing up in, which may not be the same world their parents grew up in. They must formulate a long-term goal to make a difference in that world, and they must learn how to make a realistic plan to pursue their objective. All of this is a creative task that may draw upon children's awareness of their natural dispositions—children born irreparably tone-deaf likely should not aspire to become opera singers—but that is only the start of the search for purpose. More central to the search is children's assessment of how their innermost beliefs and desires match up with some need that they have identified in the world around them. In order to make this determination, every child must observe, experiment, and reflect on the meaning of what he or she has observed. Most will find this a challenging task; but every child can do it. This is where parents come in.

Fundamental to the approach to fostering purpose in children that I am advocating is this core precept: *Whatever we do with young people counts.* Although there is no way of predicting (or controlling) just when something that we say or do will sink in, children are keen listeners and observers, and sooner or later it registers. What's more, whatever we *neglect* to say, or choose *not* to say, counts as well, again in ways that we may not always be able directly to control, predict, or detect.

Take, for example, certain words of advice that I'm sure all of us can recall having received in our early lives, which made a lasting impression. Early in my first year of high school, a crusty old English teacher named John Hawes took me to task for handing in a sloppy, half-completed assignment that revealed little more than my own laziness. My excuse (which, incredibly, I must have considered legitimate) was that I had not realized that this assignment "counted" much. Mr. Hawes fixed me in a sober gaze and said, "Mr. Damon, everything you do in this world counts."

I do not suggest that Mr. Hawes's message immediately turned my life around, or even that it struck me at the time as a profound revelation. But the idea that *things matter* did sink in, reinforced over the years by other wisdom I was exposed to, as well as by my own experience and observations. What this particular teacher said to me on that one occasion made a difference to my way of thinking about life, and it has stuck around as a kind of touchstone for me to this very day, decades later.

I can't count the number of times I've heard parents complain that their children never listen to them, or express their lack of confidence that they've had any real influence on the choices their children make. Whenever I hear this, I say that I'd be glad to bet that your kids *eventually* will reflect your influence on their values and behavior, although I can't specify exactly when or in what ways. Although no one has ever taken me up on this bet (maybe it seems too hedged by its nonspecificity), it still doesn't seem to reassure people of their potential parenting powers.

One reason that parents may have little confidence in their power to influence their children is, I think, that we often look for results too fast. A parent's influence is exerted over the long haul, and it may show up clearly only after the child has grown up and left the home. Parental influence tends to be deep but not always broad: children will make their own decisions about all kinds of things, from hairstyle to politics, while still in the long run making choices that reflect the basic values they have acquired in the course of interaction with their parents.

With this in mind, one of the most important things for parents to appreciate is that they should not seek to *directly create* a child's purpose. A parent cannot accomplish the task of identifying a purpose for a child, any more than the parent can choose the child's personality or write a script for the child's life. But a parent can introduce options. A parent can also guide a child in reflecting on the personal and social value of these options, and on how to formulate realistic plans for pursuing them. And a parent can do a world of good by supporting the choices that the child has made.

An important proviso is that parents must withhold support in cases where they are convinced that children's choices are misdirected in ways that could be destructive to themselves or others. Steering children away from harmful paths is essential.

So, with those general points about the tricky mission of parenting in mind, how specifically can parents be most effective in fostering the discovery of a sense of purpose in life?

LISTEN CLOSELY FOR THE SPARK, THEN FAN THE FLAMES

As Peter Benson, president of Search Institute in Minneapolis (the premier community-building organization for youth development), has convincingly argued, every child has a "spark" of interest buried somewhere, no matter how blasé he or she may seem when talking about everyday activities.[3] No one is in a better position than a parent to encourage a child to articulate this interest and do something about it.

Parents know their kids at least as well as anyone else; but even so, they may not know much about the dreams, aspirations, and high hopes that children so often keep hidden. When it comes to discussing future plans, parents are accustomed to doing most of the talking. For a clear view of a child's innermost aspirations, parents need to practice the conversational art of asking good questions and listening for answers.

On the subject of purpose, the interview schedule used in our research studies—included as the Appendix to this book—contains a number of good questions that are sure to evoke a child's thoughts on the matter: *What's most important to you in your life? Why do you care about those things? Do you have any long-term goals? . . . Why are these goals important to you? What does it mean to have a good life? What does it mean to be a good person? . . . If you were looking back on your life, how would you want to be remembered?* As basic as these questions may be, they are too rarely asked in dialogues between parents and their children.

A dialogue revolving around such questions triggers the kinds of reflection in a child that can lead to purposeful thoughts and actions. It also opens a window for the parent into the child's private hopes and dreams, providing rich insights about how to offer the right kinds of support.

Prominent among such insights is a better understanding of where the child is in his or her quest for purpose. Recall the groups of youth described in chapter 3: *disengaged, dreaming, dabbling,* and *purposeful.* Listening to a child's responses to questions such as those above can be wonderfully revealing as to the child's present orientation. Is the child nonpurposeful, without any sustained goals or plans beyond random, moment-to-moment impulses? Or is the child dabbling in potentially purposeful activities, but not yet grasping the meaning of these activities and coming up with good reasons to commit to them? Is the child dreaming about noble purposes without working on realistic ways to accomplish them? Or is the child already purposeful, with a clear objective that provides ultimate concerns the child believes are worth striving for?

Determining how far along the way a child has come is the first step in figuring out how to offer assistance. Taking advantage of opportunities to have a conversation that helps the child express an interest and experience a realization about how he or she might pursue that interest is vital. Often, such opportunities appear, as a surprise, when least expected. Attentive listening is crucial.

What does an effective parent-child dialogue of this kind sound like? How can a parent prod a child to open up? Here's one example, among a huge set of possibilities, of how a parent (in italics) might get a reluctant teenager talking about purpose after an uneventful day in school. This example borrows from actual dialogues that I have recorded.

What happened today in school?
I don't know, not much.
Anything interesting at all?
Not really.
Sounds like maybe you thought it was a waste of time?

Well, I guess I'm learning stuff.

What are you learning that seems important to you?

Biology is important.

Why is that important?

We saw a film in class about animals and pollution last week.

Animals and pollution?

A lot of animals are dying because of pollution, and some people are getting sick because of it; some factories are throwing it into the water, too.

Oh, I see. Have you been thinking a lot about that?

Yeah, kind of.

Why does that matter to you?

Well, you know, since I was little I've always loved animals. I started caring about animals when we got Charlie [a household pet].

Sure. I know. Is this something that you think you could get interested in learning more about?

You mean animals?

Well, how they're affected by pollution, and maybe what can be done about that.

I would like to do something about that.

Do you have any ideas about what you'd like to do?

We heard about an environmental cleanup program in Alaska that saved all the wolves there. That sounded good.

You know, if you keep being interested in this, there are lots of ways to study it and even get a job someday doing this kind of work.

I guess you need a lot of science for that.

Probably, yes. You've always done well in math and science.

Yeah, I've done okay. I know that for lots of jobs these days you need math and science.

You know there's a field of environmental science that you could study in college.

Yeah, I've been getting kind of interested in the idea of doing something about the environment, or maybe something in animal medicine.

These are good careers. They need lots of good people in them these days.

It's something I want to check out when I look at colleges, what they have in those areas.

It sounds like you're going to be a good friend to the animals one way or another.

Yeah, I guess you can either take care of the sick ones or stop them from getting sick in the first place.

Makes sense. Let's keep this in mind, if you like. Maybe there's a summer job you could apply for to see what doing these kinds of things is really like.

Okay. I can ask Mr. Henry [the science teacher] about that.

And we can ask around for you, too.

In this conversation, the parent becomes a kind of Socratic coach, drawing out the child's interests and helping make connections among the various issues that already have sparked the child's imagination. When a parent prods the child in this way to think about *something* she has found interesting in school, it helps the child gain awareness of a potential "spark" that could grow into a lasting concern. Parents should then provide the child with information that may help turn this concern into a more serious commitment, or maybe even a career path, if the child so chooses. A crucial aspect of this conversation is the delicate manner in which the parent guides the child to a set of possibilities stemming from the child's own interests and talents. In both the beginning and the end, the child makes significant statements revealing the high quality of thought about the subject that is going on in her mind; at the start, "Biology is important," and at the end, "Yeah, I guess you can either take care of the sick ones or stop them from getting sick in the first place." The parent isn't telling the child what to think; rather, the parent is helpfully steering the child toward possibilities for pursuing the fundamental interest expressed.

Of course, young people do not always announce interests in ways that are easy for parents to understand. Initial whispers of purpose are most often tentative and muted, and the child may not yet fully grasp herself that she has a developing interest in what may evolve into a source of purpose. Children are also often wary of expressing interests because they can't be certain of their parents' reaction. Picking up on these early signs of purpose is a challenge, and may lead to some frustration and what feel like missteps along the way.

The awareness every parent should start with is that the first buddings of purpose are a bit like the grass seeds that we spread around in our yards: only some will sprout, and we have no idea which ones. Fortunately, only a minuscule proportion of the seeds need to keep growing to produce a thriving lawn. The implication for cultivating purpose in the young: Parents should listen with interest to all the new ideas their children bring home, exploring whatever possibilities for developing the ideas child and parent can imagine together.

Parents are not always accustomed to being good listeners when their children toy with new ideas. We are used to giving our opinions—whether they've been solicited or not—on any topic, and we are usually ready with advice based on our own experience. Listening to a child, and engaging in a genuinely two-way conversation (or three-way, if both parents participate), is harder than lecturing; but on the plus side, I don't think many parents really enjoy lecturing much anyway.

TAKE ADVANTAGE OF REGULAR OPPORTUNITIES TO OPEN A DIALOGUE

How often do we ask young people for their opinions on matters of importance? When we're watching TV with them, for example, how often do we ask them what they thought of a news story, or of a moving or disturbing plot twist? Soliciting their thoughts is one good way to build the kind of listening habits that prepare a parent to hear early whispers of possible purposes when their children first start discovering them.

Parents do well to watch carefully for any glimmers as they spontaneously arise, but they don't need to just sit around and wait for the occasional moments when a child brings home a burning new idea. They can employ regular family occasions to trigger conversations about purpose with their children. Birthdays, holidays, and transitions, such as the start of a new school year or a change in parental employment, all can provide rich contexts for discussions about the deeper meaning of everyday events.

Once again, to be effective, parents should make sure that these conversations are two- or three-way (or many-way) dialogues, rather than simply adult-driven monologues. During such conversations, parents must learn to be good listeners and, what's more, *good interviewers*, probing children to elaborate their views, frequently asking the *Why* question, and encouraging them to think more deeply about the things they find noteworthy and interesting. When we evoke from children their own nascent ideas about what they find meaningful, we become better able to hear their first murmurs of purpose; and in this way we provide the nurturing conditions for further exploration. We can do this on their own turf, in the context of interests they have developed in school or elsewhere, or on our adult turf, in the context of family dinners, outings, and holiday get-togethers.

A traditional American holiday with especially great potential here is Thanksgiving. Unfortunately, this potential is largely wasted in that we so often use this holiday these days for little else than overeating and watching TV sports in a post-feast stupor. Thanksgiving is a built-in opportunity for family members and friends to gather and talk about what they are grateful for. Among its many other valuable psychological functions, gratitude is a window into purpose, because it helps us identify the things that we find particularly significant in our lives.[4] When we express our thanks, we increase our own awareness of what is most valuable in life, and we communicate this awareness to others around us. From gratitude springs not only an enhanced appreciation for our own blessings but also a desire to pass such blessings along to others—the heart and soul of purpose. Because Thanksgiving is a secular holiday on a national scale, everyone but emergency workers (in itself a noble purpose) is free to spend time with family or friends reflecting on the essence of gratitude, meaning, and purpose. It is hard to imagine a more ideal educational occasion for a young person's character development.

Yet, incredibly, it is amazingly difficult to turn a Thanksgiving Day family event into this kind of occasion for reflection. I have written about this before,[5] and when I'm on a speaking tour, I often grouse about it, so I won't dwell on the problem at length here. But I will note for the record that I have seen many well-intentioned and carefully crafted attempts to get children to articulate their gratitude founder upon the shoals of their impatient hunger and their parents' desires to quiet them by quickly gratifying their appetites (and—trust me—these have been quite well-fed children, bearing little risk of malnourishment were they to postpone dinner long enough to express their thanks).

Still, there are ways to salvage the situation and swim against our cultural tide of overindulgence. Some parental creativity may be called for. I attended a Thanksgiving dinner a couple of years ago where the mother, frustrated by the failure of her previous attempts to generate discussions about gratitude, asked her children and guests to come with haiku poems that they had written on the theme. It was fun, it was different, and there were only seventeen syllables to write. This parent's flash of inspiration worked beautifully. Much as parents may worry that their children won't respond to such probings (and it's true that children often won't), by steadily taking advantage of opportunities to kick off a conversation, over time more and more valuable insights will be gleaned and valuable lessons imparted.

BE OPEN-MINDED AND SUPPORTIVE OF THE
SPARKS OF INTEREST EXPRESSED

Embracing your child's interests may feel like a bit of a tug when the child is pursuing a purpose that seems strange to the parent—as in one case I observed where the daughter of two famous scientists decided to become a fashion designer. But, barring destructive or anti-social purposes, parents are wise to support children's own choices—and, what's more, to express confidence in what their child is trying to do. Not only does this improve the child's prospects for succeeding in that particular endeavor; it imparts an optimistic, can-do attitude for the long run.

A family that I have known for years spent a month at a farm with livestock. A girl in the family, age eleven—I'll call her Heather here—tended some animals at the farm. One day, Heather made a startling connection: whenever she ate hamburgers or lamb chops, the meat came from animals such as the ones she was caring for. Heather developed a passionate interest in vegetarianism, first in theory and soon thereafter in practice. She read everything she could get her hands on about how and why to exclude meats and seafood from a diet, and then she insisted that she be served strictly vegetarian meals at home and school.

Initially, Heather's parents, robust meat-eaters themselves, were not amused by the idea of preparing special food for Heather. But they were impressed by her determination and amazed at how much she learned about nutrition on her own. They encouraged her to read up on vegetarian practices at the library and questioned her at length about what she was discovering. For several years they put up with her dietary choices, insisting only that Heather plan meals that provided all the protein and other nutrients she would need as a growing adolescent. Heather extended her interest to her schoolwork, studying nutritional processes in biology, creating science projects on the topic, and writing essays about cultural food practices for social studies courses. This absorbing interest paved the way for her to become a biology major in college, later to pursue a graduate degree in public health, and so to the start of a promising career in environmental medicine. Somewhere along the way, Heather dropped her dedication to vegetarianism (she now draws the line only at red meat), but the flames of her passion for healthy eating habits, environmentally sustainable food practices, and the decent treatment of animals continue to fuel her daily efforts, providing meaning and motivation for the life and work she has chosen.

Heather's parents could never have predicted where her initial interest in vegetarianism would take her. They did recognize that something worth paying attention to was happening—a curiosity about how we live in the world, a new spark of interest in science and philosophy, a swelling of concern about something beyond the self that was disturbing her. They were intrigued by Heather's newfound dedication and burgeoning knowledge, and they wisely chose to encourage both, even though the turf she was exploring was very far from anything they cared about or were in the least bit familiar with. As it turned out, the vegetarianism itself was not destined to be Heather's final purpose: it was one of those early grass sprouts with a limited life. But it prepared the ground for a sturdier cluster of sprouts sharing many of its qualities. Today, Heather is a dedicated young woman with a clear sense of direction, shaped by her purpose as a nutritional scientist and environmental medical practitioner.

When special opportunities to encourage purpose arise spontaneously in a child's behavior, parents should pick up on them immediately, be open to them, and support them in whatever ways they can—without, though, being pushy. The child's interest should be free to take its own course, including dwindling out if that's what is destined. Parents can never know which grass seeds are going to turn out to take deep root.

CONVEY YOUR OWN SENSE OF PURPOSE AND THE MEANING YOU DERIVE FROM YOUR WORK

Parents should share their own goals and sense of purpose with their children—something that, unfortunately, they rarely get around to doing. After a hard day at work it may be more natural to complain about one's job than to talk about the parts that one finds meaningful. But it is both healthy for the parent and instructive for the child to frequently discuss in a family context the highest purpose that the parent has for the work that he or she does. This should be a touchstone for just about every conversation a parent has with a child about the subject of jobs and careers.

Parents have most likely found purpose in at least some aspect of their own jobs (or, in the case of nonworking parents, in the context of their family duties). The great majority of American workers do believe that their work is meaningful in some sense—perhaps because it helps others, perhaps because it contributes to society, perhaps because it affords a means of self-expression and personal growth, or perhaps because it provides a living for their families.[6] Work is a source of pride and purpose for most people. But how often do parents communicate that sense of pride and purpose to their children? Although I know of no formal empirical study of this question, I suspect from my own observations that the answer is hardly ever. What children so often hear instead are complaints about whatever is going wrong on the job, or joy and relief when a holiday arrives.

The complicated nature of contemporary work further obfuscates its meaning for children, who gaze at their parents' activities from the outside. As the columnist Jared Sandberg pointed out recently in the *Wall Street Journal*, today's workers more often spend their time talking on the phone or clicking on a computer than making tangible goods that a child can appreciate.[7] The child is left with the impression that the only thing that is valuable about the parent's work is the paycheck he or she brings home. Sandberg quotes the noted family scholar Stephanie Coontz: "One of the problems affluent, middle-class parents have is explaining to their kids the value of what they do, as opposed to passing along a sense of entitlement." When the child sees only the material rewards from work, he or she has no way to understand how work serves essential social needs and fulfills our personal sense of purpose. The obfuscation of work's deeper meaning is a breeding ground for apathy and cynicism, because without a positive grasp of its social and personal importance, the child will acquire a view of work as merely an unpleasant but unavoidable burden. Psychology, like nature, abhors a vacuum.

Perhaps parents feel that it would be sappy to wax on about the noble purpose of their work in front of their children. Perhaps they feel that it is too hard to explain what they do all day, and why, to children with little knowledge of complex organizations.

But for the sake of their children (and, as the positive psychology movement has taught us, for themselves as well), parents *should* bother to talk about the value of their work. It is motivating and inspiring for children to hear why their parents find their daily efforts significant. It is instructive as well: surprisingly, it is not at all obvious to children that their parents actually take pride in contributing to the world. Children may not even realize that their own healthy growth is a source of satisfaction to their parents—and this, in a very real sense, is a central part of the work of homemakers. Such feelings of pride in work must be expressed and discussed in vivid detail if children are to understand them in all their depth. This requires a frank and open disclosure of the parents' true feelings about their own purposes in life. Parents who confide in their children about such matters serve as compelling role models.

IMPART WISDOM ABOUT THE PRACTICALITIES IN LIFE

The highly purposeful young people in our studies all emanated a sense of *practical idealism*, which is to say that they knew how to accept the (hopefully temporary) limits of the possible when reality simply would not yield to their aspirations.

Such early wisdom is not inborn. Some of it can be learned through trial and error, in the course of initial, often fumbling, attempts to pursue a purpose. But parents and other mentors are also needed to provide crucial information about how the world works. No youngster can master the vast troves of our cultural knowledge, or all the complexities of our intricate social arrangements, without lots of guidance from the experienced and knowledgeable adults around them. What children learn in school barely touches the surface of the real-world knowledge they will need if they are to turn their dreams into practical action.

Parents must tell children what they know about accomplishing goals in the real world, especially the world of work.

Conveying worldly information and practical know-how is essential. Because of the unique love and respect that children feel for their parents, a parent is in a position to be the child's single most valuable source of such information. Efforts to do so can make all the difference in whether children are able to realize their ambitions. It is noteworthy how many successful people report learning about the ins and outs of career paths over family dinner conversations. Biographical accounts of powerful political dynasties such as the Kennedy clan are full of stories of extensive dinner debates between worldly-wise parents and inexperienced but eager-to-learn youngsters.[8] Recently, the writer and media personality Ben Stein has written about his life-long debt to his own knowledgeable parents: "Here I am writing this column about economics and finance. But how do I know a tiny bit about them? Because my father was a learned economist who talked about it around the dinner table, along with my mother. . . ."[9]

Stein also notes the importance of crucial social information. Parents can help children navigate the system by instructing them in proper behavioral manners, showing them how to find out about jobs or learning opportunities, and introducing them to personal connections that can enable them to get started. All these are central parts of the parental role in training children to implement their aspirations. Of course, not all parents themselves have the knowledge or experience to do this for their children—indeed, in a poignant note, Stein asks: "But what if you don't have a well-connected father . . . [or]

mother? What if you don't have a father at all? What if you are an immigrant without any connections?"

This is a question of grave moral import for our society's future. In the end, our challenge as parents is to make sure that our own children gain the social knowledge they will need to achieve their highest purposes; and our challenge as citizens is to see that all children in our society, whatever the state of their parenting, have access to the kinds of social and practical skills they will need to turn their dreams into reality. I will turn to this subject again in the last chapter.

INTRODUCE CHILDREN TO POTENTIAL MENTORS

Parents can introduce their children to other adults who might trigger sparks of interest. Our studies showed that purposeful youth often look to people outside the home for the ideas and inspiration that help them find their own purposes. Parents should actively introduce children to people who can inspire them in this way, and also support their children's mission in whatever ways they can.

The value of nonparental mentors has been well established in youth development over the past fifty years.[10] Indeed, the notion of mentoring is now so widely known and accepted that it may seem surprising that it came into general use as recently as the early 1970s. Today, successful mentoring programs such as Big Brother/Big Sister reach many thousands of children each year. These programs, naturally enough, tend to focus on deprived children who do not have all the advantages of strong family backgrounds. This is as it should be:

such children deserve all the breaks we can give them, and mentoring is a powerful way to provide needed support and guidance for any child. But I intend the phrase "any child" quite literally: mentoring provides benefits for children who are fortunate enough to have intact family environments as well. I believe it is no accident that virtually all the highly purposeful youth whom we studied had mentors outside their homes, and these mentors contributed importantly to the youngsters' quests for purpose. The mentors helped them discover, define, and pursue their quests in many ways. In the process, the youngsters acquired the capacities to successfully discover, define, and pursue purposeful missions on their own. Whenever possible, parents do well to introduce their children to people who can mentor them in such a manner.

ENCOURAGE AN
ENTREPRENEURIAL ATTITUDE

One of the defining features of highly purposeful youth is their entrepreneurial manner of pursuing objectives. For the highly purposeful people profiled in chapter 4, entrepreneurship was a stronger common factor than usual measures of success such as school achievement. Although these youngsters generally did well enough in school, few of them were valedictorians or all-A students; but virtually all were superb entrepreneurs. As a predictor of later success in life, I would place my bet on strong entrepreneurial capacities.

Cultivating an entrepreneurial spirit means encouraging the following attitudes or dispositions: (1) The ability to set clear goals and make realistic plans to accomplish them; (2) an optimistic, can-do attitude; (3) persistence in the face of obstacles and difficulties; (4) a tolerance—or more, even an appetite—for risk; (5) resilience in the face of failure; (6) determination to achieve measurable results; and (7) resourcefulness and inventiveness in devising the means to achieve those results.

Entrepreneurship is not a solitary trait but rather a cluster of characteristics that can be brought to bear on challenging tasks. When applied together, these entrepreneurial attitudes and dispositions can create powerful new ways to address problems that have long defied solutions. This is why young people who are dedicated to large purposes rely so heavily on entrepreneurial methods.

Parents can help their children develop entrepreneurial capacities by encouraging them to take on challenges and healthy risks. When voiced frequently enough, indeed as a type of parental mantra, a single four-word sentence will go a long way in sending the key message about tackling formidable tasks: *"You can do it!"* In one form or another, this kind of parental urging is a good character-building exercise. Seeking challenges, and overcoming timidity, are habits that can be acquired very early in life. When children learn to thrive on challenges rather than to avoid them, they learn a good deal about what it is possible for them to achieve.

The word "entrepreneurship" is most commonly used to refer to business concerns, but when I refer to "the entrepreneurial spirit," I mean a general orientation to life that promotes every sort of accomplishment, ranging from charity to business. Indeed, "social entrepreneurship" is the term used to refer to the application of entrepreneurial methods to the solution of social problems, and many of the highly purposeful youth profiled in chapter 4 expressed their entrepreneurship through just such causes.

Of course, children also learn a good deal that will assist them in life by engaging in entrepreneurial business activities. I hardly need to point out here the benefits of the small-scale enterprise for children who take the initiative to set one up: the celebrated lemonade stand long ago found its well-deserved niche in American legend. The annals of business success are full of stories of men and women who got their start in childhood or adolescence running a neighborhood lawn service, organizing a newspaper route, or selling Girl Scout cookies. Early business ventures of this kind, done in a motivated and industrious way, can be formative experiences that sow the seeds of entrepreneurial inclinations and know-how. Parents should encourage such activities and, just as important, they should urge their children to pursue them with the kind of entrepreneurial spirit and positive attitude described above.

One of the salutary developments in our field recently has been the emergence of an "entrepreneurial education" movement, targeting in many instances populations of high-risk youth. Children as young as eleven, many from disadvantaged homes, learn how to find business opportunities, how to market, how to mount a sales campaign, how to budget, and how to plan for growth. According to an August 2007 PBS documentary called *These Kids Mean Business,* such programs also "reactivate their interest in school—math, reading and writing in particular." For this and other reasons, the documentary's director, Zach Richter, believes that entrepreneurial education is especially well suited for disadvantaged students: "They become mentally strong. They develop initiative. . . . They're not afraid of rejection. They become comfortable with risk and ambiguity and stress." But, as he notes in his own case, early business experience benefits children from all backgrounds:

As a kid, I built a hot dog stand out of some planks of wood, a baby carriage, a large cooler, and a sterno stove. Instead of joining the local little league, I sold franks, soda and popcorn to them. My Dad took the time to teach me how to keep good records: income and expenses, profit and loss. I was an entrepreneur, though I didn't know it at the time.

Unfortunately, despite all the age-old evidence regarding the multiple benefits of early business experience, and despite the recent success of the budding entrepreneurial education movement, work-for-pay by young people has become a controversial issue in the field of youth development. Many experts have lined up against it on the basis of the threat to young people's study time. It is true that some ill-advised cases have come to light: youngsters who frequently skip classes, neglect their homework, and deprive themselves of sleep in order to earn as much spending money as possible. These are abuses that parents certainly should prevent. But a modest amount of part-time work can be instructive and morale-boosting. Work can teach youngsters productive skills and attitudes, and it can affirm for them their own value to others.

Even the oft-derided fast-food stint can be edifying when the person receives the right kind of mentoring. Recall the fast-food restaurant manager in chapter 2 who counseled his teenage employees. No matter how crabby the customer, the manager tells his young employees, "Your job is to put a smile on the customer's face."

NURTURE A POSITIVE OUTLOOK

Closely related to instilling in children a spirit of entrepreneurship is encouraging a sense of optimism. In chapter 4, we saw how young people with high purpose approach their lives with optimism and self-confidence. These powerful attitudinal strengths serve them well. Their optimism and self-confidence enable them to tackle challenges that others may find daunting or even impossible, and shield them from discouragement when things don't go their way. As I noted, many of these youngsters may have had some optimistic leanings long before they found their purposes: it is likely that genetic factors may play a role in predisposing people toward a cheerful view of life.[11] But in the long run, genetic factors can be either strengthened or overcome by experience; and in the early years, parents are the most important shapers of a child's experience.

Psychologists have made useful recommendations about how to nurture optimism and self-confidence in children, and there are a number of excellent books for parents on the subject of fostering children's emotional strengths.[12] As a general matter, parents are advised to help children interpret experiences in a hopeful manner, avoiding at all costs the kind of pessimistic "catastrophic thinking" that tends to imagine the worst thing that can possibly happen as soon as something starts to go wrong. Instead, a parent should always point out to a child how likely it is that things will turn out well, and especially *how much control* we have over how things do turn out. When problems do arise, parents should be careful to explain them in a way that avoids defeatism, panic, or blame. They should help children understand that problems are an inevitable part of life and not something to get depressed about. Indeed, that problem solving can be a great joy. An important message is that by no means does the existence of a problem mean that the child has done something wrong, or is a bad person, or is unlucky, or is destined to fail.

To convey positive attitudes to children, parents should regularly express them. I have a friend who suddenly realized that, in her home (as elsewhere), the exclamation "Just my luck!" was the standard response to bad events. Why, she wondered, were her very fortunate family members implying that their luck is usually bad? And what kind of message did this send to her children about the odds that bad things would happen to them? Thereupon, quite ingeniously I thought, my friend made a habit of correcting people who used the expression in the standard pessimistic way around her home and, what's more, went out of her way to say "Just our luck!" whenever something beneficent befell her family. This is a small step with potentially large consequences.

Everything we say and do around children registers. A child's character is formed through a succession of moment-by-moment communications and interactions with the people closest to them, and even something as simple as regularly expressing a positive outlook on life can make a significant difference.

INSTILL IN CHILDREN A FEELING OF AGENCY, LINKED TO RESPONSIBILITY

Parents should teach their children the basic principle *Whatever you do in this world matters*, and not just in the sense that it matters because their parents care about them—which is important to convey—but in the larger sense that their actions have significant consequences, for good or for bad. From the start of life, all children make an appreciable difference in the lives of the people around them. Whenever the opportunity presents itself, parents should make this clear to their children. And opportunities to point this out arise naturally all the time. For example, if a child helps with planting a garden, when the flowers begin to bloom, be sure to acknowledge the role the child played in making that happen. Or if you take your child with you to drop off a gift to an elderly person in your neighborhood, make sure to point out how much it mattered to the older person to see that the child cared.

The key principle is to take advantage of moments that arise spontaneously during conversations and such common household activities as assigning chores, getting dinner on the table, and gift-giving. *Every moment counts.* The right use of a moment here, a moment there, is sufficient for getting the message across. It is also the only feasible approach: lecturing produces little more than willful deafness (or eye-rolling). All of the occasional moments that parents use well accumulate over the years.

One of the other ways in which we can impart a sense of agency in children, the feeling that they are capable and that they are making a contribution, is to make it clear to them that you think they are interesting and capable. Although most parents treasure their children above all else, we do not always communicate our confidence in them during their everyday interactions. In many cases, parents discourage children from taking on challenges that could allow them to test their potential, and they overprotect children from risks that pose little chance of true danger. In terms of conveying that we believe that what they think about things matters, as I noted earlier, parents rarely take the time to solicit their children's views on significant issues. Nor do parents often discuss their own aspirations, thoughts, or concerns with their children, often because they are intent to make their lives as carefree as possible. Such unintended slights, ironically, are byproducts of the excessively child-centered fashion of child rearing that developed in the twentieth century and is still prevalent today. Taken to the extreme, this kind of child rearing infantilizes children by assuming that they can do little on their own and that they require constant protection to survive childhood undamaged.

One of the ways this has played out in recent years is that it is no longer common to give young people real responsibilities, such as expecting them to make regular contributions to household tasks. Obligatory tasks around the house have pretty much gone out of fashion. Instead, young people are given the freedom to spend all their time pursuing their academic studies, their soccer events and piano lessons, and their increasingly frantic personal and social schedules. The affluence that enables us to relieve youngsters of household work is certainly beneficial in some ways; and the activities that fill their schedules can certainly be worthwhile for their learning and development. But something is missing.

No longer do young people feel that they are making needed contributions to their home, that others in their family are depending on them, and that, if they fail to meet their responsibilities, they will be letting someone down or leaving some necessary task uncompleted. In addition to the character-building virtues that such responsibilities engender, there is also the key feeling of "mattering" that is not being nurtured by these missing family obligations.

Today's affluent societies will likely never go back to the time when children's efforts were needed to sustain the household economy. But even the wealthiest families can, if they choose, assign their children meaningful obligations, which teach them responsibility and endow them with a sense that what they do matters in the world. Even a young child can do something helpful, such as caring for a pet or watering the plants. And it's important that the child gets to see the results of his responsibility, or lack thereof. If the child's job is to water the plants, she should be given the chance to discover that the plants will die if she forgets to water them. (SPCA please note: I do not recommend this approach for pet care!) A few wilted plants are a reasonable price to pay for a child's character growth.

As youngsters grow older, one wonderfully effective way to impart more sense of responsibility is to get them involved in volunteering. A teenager can make a huge difference in the life of a needy child, whether through participation in a Big Brother/Big Sister type of mentoring program, or in providing an elderly person who is lonely with company. Parents should encourage this kind of voluntary work, even if it crowds out other, more self-centered activities in the daily schedule. Not only is volunteering character-building in this way; it is also a good source of sparks of interest that may develop into a life purpose, and it can teach children a great deal about the practicalities they will need to make their way in the world, as well as introducing them to potential adult mentors.

Finally, from our extensive studies of where a sense of purpose in life comes from in young people, let us summarize the set of factors that we have identified as crucial. As precepts for parents to be mindful of on a regular basis, taking advantage of all the opportunities that arise—from the smallest day-to-day moments to the more formal occasions—they bear repeating:

- Listen closely for the spark, then fan the flames
- Take advantage of regular opportunities to open a dialogue
- Be open-minded and supportive of the sparks of interest expressed
- Convey your own sense of purpose and the meaning you derive from your work
- Impart wisdom about the practicalities in life
- Introduce children to potential mentors
- Encourage an entrepreneurial attitude
- Nurture a positive outlook
- Instill in children a feeling of agency, linked to responsibility.

7

A Culture of Purpose for
All Young People

A paradoxical duality lies at the heart of nurturing youthful purpose. Young people must discover their own unique purposes, out of their own particular interests and beliefs. Yet their discoveries are guided by other people in their lives, and the purposes that they discover are inevitably shaped by values that they encounter in the culture around them. The paradox is that purpose is both a deeply individual and an unavoidably social phenomenon. It is internally constructed, yet it manifests itself in engagement with others. It is a product of inner examination and yet also of outer exploration. When a purpose is fully formed, it reflects both the genuine aspirations of the self and the practical needs of the world beyond the self.

For this reason, adults who wish to help young people find their purposes are in a somewhat awkward position. We cannot present a ready-made purpose to a young person and expect that it will suit her comfortably. We can and should, however, introduce inspiring ideas, and sources of ideas—people, books, religious or secular organizations—that may provide young people with the inspirations that will get them on their way. We also can create conditions that facilitate their own efforts to fashion purposes.

As we saw in the last chapter, parents play a vital role in this process, but they must not be left on their own. Even for children with optimal parenting, the broader society plays a decisive role. For good or for ill, our instant mass communications transmit the dominant values of our society relentlessly. A noxious or degenerate cultural environment will undermine a parent's influence, whereas a wholesome and vibrant cultural climate will bolster parental guidance. A society rich with elevated beliefs and practices encourages young people to pursue worthy aspirations and expand their sense of what they can accomplish for themselves and the world. Societies where cynicism prevails tend to demoralize young people, diminish their aspirations, and threaten their prospects for a purposeful life. Observing such a debased society decades ago, Thomas Mann wrote:

A person lives not only his own life as an individual but also the life of his epoch.... All sorts of personal aims, ends, hopes, and prospects pass before the eyes of the individual and out of these he derives the impulse to ambition and achievement. Now, if the life about him, his own time, seems to be at its core empty of food for aspirations, if he privately recognizes it to be hopeless, decrepit, meaningless... then, in such a case, a certain crippling of the personality is bound to occur.[1]

Then there is the Ben Stein question that I noted in the last chapter: What about kids whose parents don't have the resources to help their kids optimally? Most parents focus their efforts on their own kids. This is natural and understandable, but it leaves gaps in the broader society's ability to provide the right conditions for all young people's quests for purpose. What about kids who aren't lucky enough to have attentive parents? What about kids who don't have functioning parents at all? These kids need support from other sources. A decent society provides such support, because all young people deserve the chance for a purposeful life. What's more, if neglected youth don't find positive purposes to dedicate themselves to, they may pursue less constructive activities that will come back to haunt their society. A society that provides a culture of purpose for its young people creates public institutions that offer mentoring, presenting a positive vision of the purposeful life as well as the practical knowledge needed to pursue that life.

Building such a society does not require any sort of Utopian dreaming or heavy-handed system of governmental directives. Rather, a culture of purpose must be built—and continually rebuilt—in multiple small ways, by both individuals and institutions, that take responsibility for the values they present through their words, their deeds, and the examples they set. Government, especially at the local level, certainly can play a constructive role by partnering with these individuals and institutions; but it cannot foster youth purpose through top-down programs or coercive legislation. A culture of purpose cannot be enforced.

Nor are there material prerequisites for a culture of purpose. We know that young people have found purpose all through the ages, in good times or bad, in times of plenty and in times of economic deprivation. During the Great Depression of the 1930s, families held together; young people helped out as needed; and many of these young people grew up to be highly effective, responsible citizens who contributed greatly to society.[2] Wars, epidemics, famines, hard times of every imaginable sort have served as tolerable breeding grounds for a sense of purpose among those who have endured them. We can be sure that the youth who did adapt successfully to those difficult conditions found guidance and inspiration in some exemplary people around them and in the larger culture of purpose that those people represented.[3]

COMMUNITY BUILDING FOR YOUTH PURPOSE

The closest thing to a prerequisite for a culture of purpose is a sense of community. When parents, teachers, and other adults in children's lives share a sense of community, they reinforce each other's efforts.

I have seen this in action. About ten years ago, I participated in a number of town meetings dedicated to creating the most conducive climate for raising the young. The idea behind this work, which I wrote about in my book *The Youth Charter: How Communities Can Work Together to Raise Standards for All Our Children,* is that young people do best in places where adults present them with high expectations that are clear and coherent.[4] In meetings that included parents, teachers, town officials, clergy, sports coaches, and representatives of the local news media, I observed intense discussions about how to marshal the town's resources in order to promote healthy youth development. To the surprise of many who took part in these discussions, coming to agreement about the standards adults should aim to promote in young people was never difficult: the goals widely shared were that children should acquire character virtues such as honesty, compassion, respect, and moral courage, and that they should develop competence in school, work, and essential life skills. Groups of adults can be highly effective in coming together to transmit those values to the next generation, and in doing so a sense of community is born.

In the course of the youth charter work that I did, I saw many dedicated citizens reach out to help young people all across communities, most often by ensuring that a town had the capacity to provide positive activities and mentoring for all its young. Sometimes, it was a matter of new resources—opening a computer-oriented branch of the library, creating a youth radio show on a local FM channel—and other times it was more a matter of bolstering and coordinating resources that already existed, such as switching a soccer league from Sunday mornings so that the kids who wanted to go to church did not have to make a choice between the two.

All these efforts required leadership and a great deal of individual initiative from the parents in town (my own role was limited to facilitating the discussion and observing the results). They were able to make a marked impact on the town's capacity to serve its youth; and in the process, the participants became inspiring examples of civic engagement for the young, which is a highly rewarding role to play. Such efforts, however, are time-limited: they need to be constantly renewed by new generations of parents and citizens as the older generation moves past its own child-raising years. Taking some of the burden off individuals is also important, and those who are interested in spearheading such efforts in their own community should take heart that a number of organizations have been founded to provide direction and support.

THE POSITIVE APPROACH TO
COMMUNITY DEVELOPMENT

One such effort has been led by Peter Benson, president of the Search Institute in Minneapolis, Minnesota, mentioned earlier. The Search Institute works with communities around the world to help them identify the "assets" that promote healthy youth development. The assets are both internal to the child (qualities of character and competence) and external in the resources that the community is able to provide (family, educational, recreational, religious, and so on). Benson and his colleagues help communities build their own leadership and create their own programs.

There are two things that I particularly like about the Search Institute approach. First, unlike the usual "branded" programs that play off the fame (and egos) of their founders, the Search work is so thoroughly absorbed into the community that it quickly becomes practically invisible. I discovered this firsthand when a niece of mine phoned me excitedly to talk about some important community-building work she had taken on as part of a high school project. The class had gone out into the community to "map" the "assets" that were available to young people, including reliable places where kids could spend their spare time, places where they could play sports and learn skills, places where they could get job training or religious instruction, and so on. She talked at length, and with a distinctly noticeable sense of purpose, about ideas that she had for identifying and bolstering the community's resources in order to make them available to kids all over town. She and her friends had assumed leadership of major components of the project. In fact, their sense of ownership was so solid that she had no awareness of the Search Institute or its role in triggering this initiative in her town. Only by clicking on link after link of the school's Web site did I finally confirm what I had suspected from the language my niece used to describe the activities that had so inspired her—that this, indeed, was a Search Institute project. The invisibility of Search's role had enabled my niece to participate in a way that engendered an authentic sense of purpose of her own.

The second feature that I like about the Search Institute's approach to community building is its unrelentingly positive vision of young people and their potential value to society. In stark contrast to youth programs that start with a focus on the troubles that young people can get into, and unavoidably end up viewing such people as problems that need to be somehow "cured," the Search approach starts by identifying the positive assets that every young person has. In his writings, Benson has criticized the "deficit reduction" view that long has dominated professions that serve youth. The vision of young people as clusters of risks to be avoided (substance abuse, premature pregnancy, emotional disturbance) or problems to be solved (learning disabilities, underachievement, unruly conduct) is an essentially defeatist vision that can never be helpful. An absence of problems is not sufficient for a purposeful, fulfilled life.

I myself can vouch for both the dominance and the depressing effect of such a "deficit reduction" approach. When I came to Stanford ten years ago to take over the directorship of its Center on Adolescence, I was greeted by a series of dramatic posters lining the walls of the building. Each poster screamed a warning about the dangers young people posed to themselves and others. Although I can't remember the exact messages (since I had the posters removed within the week), they contained such statements as: "Do you know that thousands of young people will commit murder this year?" "Do you know that one in three youngsters will start smoking [or drinking or taking drugs] this year?" "Do you know that young people cause most of the fatal traffic accidents in many parts of the country?" "Do you know that most teenage pregnancies lead to single parenthood?" No doubt, all the statistics were correct, and they definitely pointed to worrisome problems; but they certainly didn't constitute the most productive starting place for thinking about the potentials of youth development.

The "positive youth development approach" pioneered by Benson, Richard Lerner of Tufts University, and a few other like-minded scientists has by now gained advocates throughout the field.[5] Researchers and practitioners have found it to be far more effective than approaches that focus on what's wrong with kids. While the positive approach recognizes the developmental challenges that young people face, it refuses to view the developmental process mainly as an effort to overcome deficits and risk. Instead, it emphasizes the manifest potential of youth—including those from the most disadvantaged backgrounds, as well as those with highly troubled personal histories. The positive youth approach aims at understanding, educating, and engaging children in productive activities rather than at correcting, curing, or treating them for maladaptive tendencies or so-called disabilities.

The work of Benson, Lerner, and other researchers has paved the way for more pointed efforts to help *all* young people find their purposes in life. In order for our society at large to most effectively foster these efforts, research has identified a core set of methods we should follow. At the societal level, these principles help establish a general culture of purpose that reaches everyone growing up in that society.

SETTING THE STAGE FOR A CONFIDENT, CAN-DO OUTLOOK

As we noted in the last chapter, four of the most valuable words that can come out of a parent's mouth are "You can do it!" Societies, of course, don't have mouths *per se*; but they do transmit messages all the same. In recent times, our society has chosen *not* to send every child the message that he or she "can do it." Quite the contrary: with each passing year, we seem to find new ways to let kids know that life is full of risks and hardships that they can't handle without our persistent aid and vigilance.

As the parent of three children, I certainly understand the tremendous fear that the thought of an injured child can arouse. But our physical protectiveness of children has reached so deeply into their routine activities that one wonders if we are actually training them for timidity—not exactly the best way to protect them as they prepare for later life. By 2007, virtually all playgrounds in the United States had been stripped of their monkey bars, dodgeball had been banned from school gym programs, and—perhaps to prove that there is always a new frontier for every foolish mania—one school in Colorado forbade "tag" during recess.[6] It is one thing to warn children about playing in traffic, and another thing entirely to prohibit activities that, in all but freak incidents, lead to little more than bumps and bruises. (And even considering the freak incidents, do we really want kids to grow up avoiding every minor probability of danger, from nature hikes to air travel?) What kinds of messages are such prohibitions sending children about what they are able to handle in life?

We are also sending negative messages by pathologizing our children. Increasing numbers in recent years have been diagnosed as "learning disabled," a disparaging and misleading label that wields enormous influence over how a child is perceived, treated, and medicated. Some children are labeled in this way mainly because they exhibit emotional restlessness of the sort that, in a less child-protective culture, is routinely taken care of as a normal disciplinary matter. The label "disabled" itself can become self-fulfilling, since children are acutely aware of how they are being appraised, and they base their own self-conceptions largely on how others see them.[7] Our use of this labeling for ever larger segments of the population (especially boys) indicates a more general tendency to perceive children as fragile and inept creatures, who need constant protection from the ordinary challenges of everyday living.[8]

There is no question that our society should do its utmost to see that all children have as many advantages as it is humanly possible to grant them, including medical and psychological services when they can be truly helpful. But there will always be limitations of nature, health, economics, family background, and other conditions in the child's life that elude our inevitably imperfect control. The fact is that children thrive on challenges, and they learn to handle the world in a competent and confident manner by taking healthy risks. One of the best child-rearing tips I have heard comes from Maria Shriver, who commented on a media show that she would advise children to do one thing each day that frightens them—and I'm sure she meant things that are quite safe, but challenging.[9] The point is not to expose children unnecessarily to scary experiences, but rather to teach them to deal confidently with whatever life has in store for them.

Most important, children must not develop the habit of avoiding difficulties out of fear that they will not be able to deal with them.

Pursuing any purpose surely entails some hard moments. The good news is that every child, in his or her own way, is capable of making such a commitment. No child who retains a living brain is ever wholly or permanently disabled. Whatever the condition, there are always useful and self-fulfilling things that the child can learn to do. Encouraging children to make the effort expands their range of learning and increases their motivation to do more. Assuming that a task is too hard restricts the child's potential and discourages him.

No society can solve its so-called youth problems by dwelling on how hard it is to be a child in today's world—or, for that matter, on how hard it is to be a child without certain key advantages. This is where the good news from positive youth development research comes in: We know that children can survive—and thrive—in the hardest of circumstances. The children most likely to thrive are those who move toward positive goals without letting hardships deter them. These are the *purposeful* children, the ones who are discovering that a good offense is also the best defense against disabling attitudes in the world around them. For our part, we should not leave such discoveries to chance. We must always examine how we as a society treat our children, making sure that the activities we urge on them demonstrate our strong confidence in their abilities and our expectations for their success.

SCHOOLS WITH PURPOSE

In a misguided effort to spur student achievement, schools have narrowed their focus to language and math skills and have put pressure on teachers to improve scores on standardized, bubble-checking types of tests. The results have been predictable. Some children do fine, as they would in practically any learning context; others struggle with the standardized formats and lose interest in academic learning altogether. The majority muddle through with mediocre performances and little understanding of why they are being taught the material that their teachers present to them. As for the teachers, they feel forced to spend their time "teaching to the test." Recently, two educational leaders—Chester Finn and Diane Ravitch, no slouches when it comes to academic rigor—acidly commented: "We're at risk of turning U.S. schools into test-prepping skill factories where nothing matters except exam scores on basic subjects."[10]

Not only does the single-minded focus on test taking restrict teachers' judgments about how and what students should learn; it crowds out time for discussing such broader questions as what a person can and should do with academic knowledge in the world beyond school—the all-important question of the *purpose* of learning.

If we are turning our public schools into places where, as Finn and Ravitch write, "nothing matters" other than meaningless test taking, we are stripping schools of their capacities to inspire purpose. The authors point out that this situation is not even good for what it intends to accomplish, national economic competitiveness; and, beyond that, it misses the boat entirely for the urgent task of educating for citizenship: "We need schools that prepare our children to excel in the global workforce but also as full participants in our society, our culture, our polity and our economy."[11]

Above all, schools must address the *Why* question with students about all that they do. Why do people study academic subjects? Why is it important to read and write? To spell words correctly? (This not only helps students better understand the purpose of schooling but also exposes them to a respected adult's own quest for purpose.) Why do we have rules against cheating? (This is a good way to convey moral standards such as honesty, fairness, and integrity—and again, it is a missed opportunity in most schools, even those with strong character education agendas.) Why are you, and your fellow students, here at all?

Every part of the curriculum should be taught with the *Why* question squarely in the foreground. Finn and Ravitch believe that the humanities are especially well suited for this ("History and literature also impart to their students . . . the ability to question, to ask both "why?" and "why not?").[12] But I have found in my own work that instruction in the hard sciences also offers a vivid context for raising questions; and, as an added benefit, such questions spur students' interest in often obscure subject matter by adding excitement to the material. Some years ago, I was given a chance to try this idea out during a summer school program for gifted students. We discussed recent research in microbiology and the ethical questions that raised, such as the social desirability of cloning. Students tore into their difficult scientific lessons with zest, motivated at least in part by their enhanced appreciation of the enormous moral issues at stake.

If schools are to live up to their role in preparing students to be "full participants in our society," they must also teach them how to engage in their communities as active citizens, and they must teach them how to operate in a political democracy. On the first matter—community involvement—American schools have done a fairly good job over the past decade, inducing students to participate in community service with considerable success. One survey showed that over 50 percent of high school students perform community service at least monthly, and more than 25 percent do so weekly.[13] But there is much more that we must do on the civic engagement front.

In particular, political knowledge and interest among today's young is so low that we have good reason to worry about the future of our democracy. This problem cannot be reduced to voting patterns—in fact, there was an upswing in youth voting during the 2004 election. But civic life (running for local office, attending neighborhood meetings, participating in committees) has dropped so far off the radar screen for young adults that it barely appears in surveys of how they spend their time.[14] We have seen how surveys show that most young people have little admiration for civic and political leaders and perceive no role for themselves in governing our society. In every survey I know, adolescents and young adults express dramatically lower levels of civic spirit than any other cohort. For example, in one poll conducted by AARP and reported in July 2006, 74 percent of adults over fifty identified themselves as highly patriotic, in contrast to only 34 percent of young people in the age range 18–34.[15] Social scientists have estimated that there has never been a time in American history when so small a proportion of young people between the ages of twenty and thirty have sought or accepted leadership roles in governmental or civic organizations.

Today's youth don't believe that they can make a difference, and they haven't thought much about the kind of difference they would like to make if they could. Indeed, it seems that many of them know so little about our political system that they don't even know where they would get started.

Anne Colby and her colleagues at the Carnegie Foundation for the Advancement of Teaching have studied this problem at the college level. The Carnegie group notes that college students are much more likely to participate in community service than in political activities. No doubt, this is a result of the situation described above: our public schools have had success in fostering community involvement but have not done much to educate students for political understanding and active citizenship in a democratic society. Due to students' lack of knowledge about how to participate, they tend to be skeptical that they could accomplish anything worthwhile in the political realm. The Carnegie study found that students make such statements as "We don't see the relevance of politics for our lives," and "We don't trust politicians or the political process."[16]

But Colby and her colleagues also found that the right kinds of college courses and programs can change these attitudes and impart the knowledge students need to make sound political judgments. When offered courses and extracurricular activities that reveal how a democracy actually works, students gain the necessary knowledge and motivation to participate. And what's more, the students who show the least interest initially are the ones who benefit most. The Carnegie group recommends that both secondary schools and higher education should pay as much attention to promoting political engagement as they have to encouraging community service. Although this research focuses on higher education, the group's recommendations are even more pertinent to education at the secondary school level, where students' early understanding and attitudes about political engagement are formed.

POSITIVE ROLE MODELS IN THE
PUBLIC SPHERE

The right kinds of educational opportunities in school must be reinforced by positive examples beyond school. Young people are always watching adults for cues about what's worth pursuing and how best to pursue it. If the adults tend to be cynical and self-serving, we can be sure children will take that as a cue. Unfortunately, we live in a time when many public officials have set terrible examples. The idea that public officials should provide admirable role models for young people actually has been discounted by recent political commentators. After one of the seemingly endless scandals of recent years, a prominent blogger offered the following view of politicians and public officials: "There is always a taint of, if not corruption, then compromise about them. This idea that they are moral leaders is moronic."[17] And a *New York Times* columnist noted that she wants leaders to pass good laws and make sensible decisions. With a thoroughly modern tone of resignation, she wrote, "We do not hire our elected officials to shape our children's characters."[18]

If this is our predominant perception of our political leaders today, and if we have resigned ourselves to the idea that they may symbolize unethical behavior, is it any wonder that students are uninspired by mainstream politics? It is true that we do not "hire" political leaders primarily to shape children's characters; and yet we have the right to expect that acting as an honorable role model should be a necessary part of any civic leader's job description. Political leadership, after all, is not simply a matter of performing certain tasks and services: at least as important is the public spirit that the leader promotes, and it is far from "moronic" to hope that our leaders will promote a moral public spirit. There is no question that young people keenly observe those who have status and power in their society, and that their own attitudes and behavior are strongly influenced by what they see.[19]

Compounding the problem, the news media often sensationalize the scandalous behavior of political leaders rather than reporting it in a responsible manner. The "gotcha!" ethic of today's journalism may or may not sell newspapers: there are doubts about this in the industry, especially given declining circulation figures. But there is little doubt that such reporting leads to what one media critic has called a "spiral of cynicism" about political engagement that has spread throughout our society. Again, it is young people just forming their first impressions of the social world and those who govern it who are most affected.

What's more, the problem extends far beyond the political realm. The mass media too often characterize corporate business as nothing more than a self-serving exercise in greed, carried out in as corrupt and ruthless a manner as its leaders can get away with. In television and movies, people in business are most often characterized by avarice, dishonesty, or downright villainy. One study of how television portrays corporate leaders found that "a majority of the CEO's portrayed on prime time have committed felonies," and that Hollywood generally portrays such leaders in a disparaging rather than admiring light.[20] In other sectors of our society, media stories commonly spotlight the foibles of sports stars, artistic celebrities, and other prominent cultural icons—although, at the same time, the media glamorizes these same celebrities, conveying a truly mixed message to young viewers.

None of this plays a constructive role in a young person's search for purpose: indeed, as they look for positive role models, young people these days had better keep their eyes averted from the media that dominate mass communications. In any democratic society, it is important that media members do their jobs and report everything the public needs to know to make informed decisions. Reporters who write about public affairs honestly and courageously themselves become positive role models in citizenship for the young. But when the balance shifts from vigorous investigation to self-serving sensationalism, young people see through it and stop taking the reporting seriously. Not only does this breed cynicism; it also persuades them that they will find few, if any, positive role models in the public sphere.

If young people are to aspire to become active citizens in the fullest sense of the term, the public figures they observe must emanate a sense of purpose and act in ways that are not transparently self-serving. The same standard applies to leaders in every occupation visible to the public. This cannot, of course, be regulated beyond basic legal standards (which, even if more minimal than the standards referred to here, some still have had trouble abiding by). Admirable public behavior must become a matter of personal awareness and conscience. Public figures must understand and accept their responsibility to set positive examples. They must recognize the influence that their actions have on the younger generation, who always will be watching; and they must tailor their own speech and conduct accordingly.[21] They also should make efforts to communicate their own sense of purpose, answering with clarity and candor questions about whatever goals they are trying to accomplish. If Internet, print, and broadcast accounts of our society's influential people were focused on what matters to them and why, rather than on their misdeeds and peccadilloes, the veil of cynicism that obstructs young people's view of what it means to be a full citizen in a democratic society would start to lift.

LOOKING PAST THE CULTURE OF SHORT HORIZONS TO A CULTURE OF NOBLE PURPOSE

In many ways, this has been a book about benign yet shortsighted and misplaced intentions. Our efforts to goad our children toward success have fallen short of granting them genuine happiness because we have placed far too much emphasis on superficial and transitory markers of success rather than on enduring, life-fulfilling goals. Our efforts to protect our children from the real and imagined hazards of daily existence have limited their horizons and curtailed their acquisition of skills they will need when they hit the real world. Our efforts to force schools to "produce" higher test scores have robbed schools of their capacities to instill a broader vision of the world and a robust motivation to learn, the kind of vision and motivation that students will need long after their school years are over. This shortsighted approach has sabotaged every possible enlightened aim that we might have for our children. Economically, it prepares them poorly for the globalized world that is defining their epoch. Psychologically, it sows seeds of pessimism, uncertainty, and self-doubt. Morally, it opens the door to a selfish and cynical worldview based on little more than materialistic craving. Socially, it engenders civic disengagement and undermines citizenship. Long term, neither the individual child nor the society at large can emerge as the winner.

Yet in every time and place, including our own, there are many young people who thrive with purpose. They find their own paths to fulfillment and happiness, often guided by adults who introduce young people to purposes that inspire them. If this book sounds cautionary notes about young people who are drifting or discouraged, it also offers notes of hope in its portrayal of young people who are striving to meet their full potential. The population of young people today is a wildly mixed lot: some are thriving with purpose; some don't seem to care at all about anything purposeful; a few (the deeply disturbed) are dedicating themselves to destructive ends; and most (the majority of young people in our study) are doing or thinking about activities that could lead in a purposeful direction, but are having difficulty making a sustained commitment to any of them.

The implications here should be clear to every reader of this book. The young people who have started dabbling in potentially purposeful activities can be encouraged to think more about what these activities contribute to the world and how they can bring meaning to their own lives. The young people who are dreaming about great possibilities can be helped to focus on accomplishments that they actually will be able to achieve, and they can be taught how to make realistic plans to reach their goals. Young people who express little interest in anything beyond themselves can be shown the rewards of commitment and the perils of disengagement. Young people who are confused, or dedicated to goals that may lead in antisocial directions, can be engaged in caring moral relationships that impart to them a clear sense of right and wrong. In such ways, every child can be pointed toward choices that will lead him or her to a life of noble purpose.

Ultimately, all young people will make their own choices: no one can do this for them. But we can make it far more likely that they will be able to make good choices which provide them with a lifelong sense of well-being. We can offer them possibilities that fire their imaginations, guidance that encourages their highest aspirations, support that helps them realize their aspirations, and a cultural climate that inspires rather than demoralizes them. There is no young person who cannot be uplifted by this kind of attention. The path to purpose is available to everyone, and by helping all young people to find it, we ensure a hopeful future for the entire society.

APPENDIX:
Questionnaire from the Youth Purpose Study

Author's note: This is the questionnaire we used in interviewing young people for the Youth Purpose Study. Such questions may be of interest as starting points for launching conversations that can help to identify young people's interests and guide them.

I. Introduction:
    a. Tell me a little about yourself. What kind of person are you?

    b. What kinds of things do you really care about? Why do you care about these things?

    c. What's most important to you in your life? Why is that important to you?

This is the form of the interview that our research team used in the initial wave of studies (2003–2006) discussed in this book. We have revised and updated the interview for follow-up studies that we are now conducting. We also have developed a survey method for sampling large numbers of young people. Researchers who are interested in obtaining details of our current methods may request them by e-mailing to Lisa Staton (staton@stanford.edu).

d. Do you have any long-term goals? What are a few of the more important ones? Why are these goals important to you?

> *If no,* That's interesting, why do you prefer not to have goals? / What does it mean to you not to have goals?
>
> *If yes,* Are you doing anything now to achieve these goals or objectives? *If yes,* What are you doing? *If no,* What has kept you back from doing something to meet these goals?

e. What does it mean to have a good life?

f. What does it mean to be a good person?

g. What would you say you spend most of your energy on these days?

h. If you were looking back on your life, how would you want to be remembered? What would you want to be remembered for? Why?

II. Inspiration of purpose/formative experiences:

a. Earlier you talked about [x] being important to you. Can you tell me how and why this became important? When did it become important to you?

b. Why did you get involved with this particular objective or cause rather than with a different one?

c. Is there someone who helped you act on your goal(s) initially?

d. Would you say your friends and family are concerned with the same things? Have your friends, family and other people in your life generally supported or opposed your efforts?

e. Have you gotten others involved in your efforts? *If yes,* how did you do this?

f. Apart from particular people, were there other things that influenced you (books, films, particular experiences, or other things)?

III. Opportunities and supports for maintenance of purpose:
a. Do you look up to anyone?
b. Do you have a mentor? Are there qualities in this mentor, or in others, that you admire?

IV. Obstacles, pressures and rewards:
a. Has it been hard for you to remain dedicated to this aim? Will it be difficult for you to remain committed down the road?
b. (*If yes to a*) What were the obstacles? How did you overcome them?

V. Future goals and responsibilities:
a. Are there qualities that you possess that helped you in achieving the goals that are important to you? Are there qualities that you possess that have made it more difficult?
b. Picture yourself at, say, 40 years of age. What will you be doing? Who will be in your life? What will be important to you? What will be going on in the area that concerns you?
c. What are your plans in the immediate future, say the next few years?

VI. Categories of purpose:
a. Tell me about your friends and family.
b. How important are they to you relative to the other things in your life? Why?

c. Do you want to have a family of your own someday? Why? How important is that to you? Why?

d. Do you do anything special to show your family or friends that they are important to you? *If yes,* what do you do? Why?

e. What role does religion, faith, spirituality, or God play in your life, if any? Are you active in a church or organized religion? What kinds of things do you do there?

f. Is your community important to you? How does it play a role in your life? Do you do anything to help improve your community? Do you do any community service? *If yes,* what do you do? Why do you do it?

g. Are you an American citizen? What does it mean to you to be a citizen? Is it important to you to be a citizen? Why or why not?

h. When you get older, what kind of work would you like to do? Why? Will your career be important to you? Why? How important will it be? Why? Are you doing anything now to prepare you for your life's work/career?

VII. Closing:

a. We're coming to the end of the interview; is there anything you would like to add about what's important to you or what you are trying to accomplish in life?

b. Summing up, what do you think matters most to you at this time? Will that still matter most to you as you get older? Why/Why not?

NOTES

PREFACE

1. Anne Colby and William Damon, *Some Do Care: Contemporary Lives of Moral Commitment* (New York: Free Press, 1992).

2. My collaborators on "The Good Work Project" are Howard Gardner and Mihaly Csikszentmihalyi. See H. Gardner, M. Csikszentmihalyi, and W. Damon, *Good Work: When Excellence and Ethics Meet* (New York: Basic Books, 2001), and also goodworkproject.org.

3. The "traveling curriculum" project was done in collaboration with The Project for Excellence in Journalism and The Committee for Concerned Journalists (journalism.org).

4. Our studies in youth purpose are far from over: we are in the midst of an extensive program of data collection and analysis which we expect will substantially add to and refine the first round of conclusions discussed in this book.

5. See Christopher Peterson and Martin Seligman, *Character Strengths and Virtues: A Handbook and Classification* (New York: Oxford University Press, 2004).

CHAPTER 1

1. The average age of marriage in the United States has risen five years over the past half century, and the trend is sharper in other industrial nations. Moreover, it seems to be accelerating everywhere.

2. Jeffrey Arnett, *Emerging Adulthood: The Winding Road from the Late Teens to the Twenties* (New York: Oxford University Press, 2004), p. 6.

3. U.K. Parliamentary Archives, 2002.

4. Nadira Hira, "You Raised Them, You Manage Them!" *Fortune* magazine, May 28, 2007, 38–44.

5. Jason Ryan Dorsey, *My Reality Check Bounced* (New York: Broadway Books, 2007).

6. As a life phase, adolescence is a response to modern social environments that offer individuals a variety of choices as to how to shape their future. Faced with choices about what work they will do, whom (or even whether) they will marry, and what they will worship or believe, young people in the modern world often take some time before they establish life commitments. It was not until 1904 that a psychologist (G. Stanley Hall) named this preparatory period "adolescence." Thus, in a scientific sense, the transitional life phase of adolescence is little

more than a century old, and in a social sense it probably is not much older than that.

7. See William Damon, Foreword, in Richard Lerner and Laurence Steinberg, eds., *Handbook of Adolescent Psychology* (New York: John Wiley, 2004), pp. vii–viii.

8. Erik Erikson, *Youth: Identity and Crisis* (New York: W. W. Norton, 1968).

9. The data reported in this book come mostly from the first phase of our study, completed in 2006. Data collection will continue at least through the year 2009, and we will report new findings as they emerge from our analyses over the coming years.

10. With the exception of some of the highly purposeful youth described in chapter 4, I have changed the names and certain identifying features of all the subjects quoted in this book.

11. See Martin Seligman, *Authentic Happiness: Using the New Positive Psychology to Realize Your Potential for Lasting Fulfillment* (New York: Free Press, 2002).

12. Jessica was not a subject in the research studies cited in this chapter and later in the book (especially in chapters 3 and 4). She, and a few other examples presented for the sake of illustration, are drawn from my personal acquaintance or other observations. In such instances, I have changed names and certain identifying features.

13. Anthony Seldon, "It Is Worthwhile Teaching Children Well-being," *Financial Times,* June 25, 2007, 13:5.

14. Madeline Levine, *The Price of Privilege: How Parental Influence and Material Advantage Are Creating a Generation of Discon-*

nected and Unhappy Kids (New York: HarperCollins, 2006), p. 5.

15. Laura Pappano, "The Incredibles," *New York Times, Education Life Section,* Jan. 7, 2007, pp. 7–12.

16. Alan J. Schwartz, "Four Eras of Study of College Student Suicide in the United States: 1920–2004," *Journal of the American College of Health,* vol. 54, no. 6 (2006), pp. 353–66. Schwartz reports over 1,400 suicides by college and university students in the fourteen-year period ending in 2004. A rule of thumb among counselors is that about ten people attempt suicide for each "successful" act. It is also well known in the suicide literature that reported data are highly uncertain, since many suicides, especially among higher-status people, are not disclosed. See Ann Haas, Herbert Hendlin, and John Mann, "Suicide in College Students," *American Behavioral Scientist,* vol. 46, no. 9 (2003), pp. 1224–40.

17. "Suicides Increased by 8% in the 10 to 24 Age Group," *Wall Street Journal,* September 7, 2007, p. B 4.

18. Barbara Schneider and David Stevenson, *The Ambitious Generation: Motivated But Directionless* (New Haven: Yale University Press, 2000), p. 8.

19. PBS, *Declining by Degrees* (2005), a John Merrow Production.

20. Kenneth Keniston, *The Uncommitted: Alienated Youth in American Society* (New York: Harcourt, Brace, & World, 1965), p. 17.

21. In this regard, *The Uncommitted* trod a similar path to Paul Goodman's *Growing Up Absurd,* published in 1960, around the time when Keniston was finishing his research. Goodman's nonempirical examination of growing up in America offers a critique of the society from the viewpoint of young people con-

fronted with the various hypocrisies and bad values embedded in the culture. Whatever one thinks about the validity of the critique, there is no question that the youthful protagonists Goodman had in mind were a smart and sensitive lot, prone to cerebral examinations of their surroundings. This keenly critical youthful persona had long been common in fiction (e.g., Holden Caulfield in J. D. Salinger's *Catcher in the Rye*). Goodman introduced the persona to the world of sociological analysis and critique, and Keniston turned the lens of empirical social science on it. But both studies were representing a select and rarified perspective.

22. Arnett, *Emerging Adulthood,* p. 3.

23. William Damon, *Greater Expectations: Overcoming the Culture of Indulgence in Our Homes and Schools* (New York: Free Press, 1996).

CHAPTER 2

1. Rick Warren, *The Purpose-Driven Life* (Grand Rapids, MI: Zondervan, 2003).

2. Vittorio Gallese, Morris Eagle, and Paolo Migone, *Intentional Attunement: Mirror Neurons and the Neural Underpinnings of Interpersonal Relations,* University of Padua, 2005; M. Jacobini et al., "Grasping the Intentions of Others with One's Own Mirror Neuron System," *PLOS Biology* (2005), 529–35.

3. P. B. Baltes, U. Lindenberger, and U. M. Staudinger, "Life Span Theory in Developmental Psychology," in W. Damon and R. M. Lerner, eds., *Handbook of Child Psychology, Vol. 1.*

Theoretical Models of Human Development, 6th ed. (New York: Wiley, 2006), 569–664.

4.   See E. Werner and R. Smith, *Journeys from Childhood to Midlife: Risk, Resilience, and Recovery* (Ithaca, NY: Cornell University Press, 2001).

5.   Erikson, *Youth: Identity and Crisis* (New York: W. W. Norton, 1994).

6.   C. D. Ryff and B. Singer, "Middle Age and Well-Being," *Encyclopedia of Mental Health* (New York: Academic Press, 1998), 707–19.

7.   See, e.g., C. Peterson and M. Seligman, *Character Strengths and Virtues: A Handbook and Classification* (New York: Oxford, 2003).

8.   Daniel Kahneman, "Experienced Utility and Objective Happiness: A Moment-Based Approach," in Daniel Kahneman and Abraham Tversky, eds., *Choices, Values and Frames* (New York: Cambridge University Press and the Russell Sage Foundation, 2000), 673–92.

9.   Ibid.

10.   D. McAdams, "Generativity in Midlife," in M. Lachman, ed., *Handbook of Midlife Development* (New York: John Wiley, 2001), 395–443.

11.   W. Damon, J. Menon, and K. Bronk, "The Development of Purpose in Adolescence," *Journal of Applied Developmental Science,* 7 (2003), 119–28.

12.   Bonnie Benard, *Fostering Resiliency in Kids: Protective Factors in the Family, School and Community* (San Francisco: Far West Laboratory, 1991).

13.   See, e.g., Timothy Burns, *From Risk to Resilience: A Journey*

with Heart for Our Children, Our Future (Marco Pao Publishers, 1994).

14. Ronald Dahl, "Adolescent Brain Development: A period of vulnerabilities and opportunities," *Annals of the N.Y. Academy of Sciences,* 1021 (2004), 1–22.

15. Ibid.

16. Mihaly Csikszentmihalyi, *Finding Flow: The Psychology of Engagement with Everyday Life* (New York: Basic Books, 1997).

17. Damon, Menon, and Bronk, "The Development of Purpose in Adolescence."

18. See, e.g., Robert Emmons, *The Psychology of Ultimate Concerns: Motivation and Spirituality in Personality* (New York: Guilford Press, 1999).

19. See S. Strauss, "Developmental Change," in William Damon, ed., *Handbook of Child Psychology,* 5th ed. (New York: Wiley, 1998).

20. As part of our study of moral exemplars, we interviewed twenty theologians and other scholars, from a wide variety of ideological perspectives, about how to define the difference between noble and ignoble ends. The results of these interviews are the basis of my conclusions here. For the entire set of results, see chapter 2 of Colby and Damon, *Some Do Care: Contemporary Lives of Moral Commitment*.

21. J. Haidt, *The Happiness Hypothesis: Finding Modern Truth in Ancient Wisdom* (New York: Basic Books, 2006).

22. J. Haidt, "The Emotional Dog and Its Rational Tail: A social intuitionist approach to moral judgment," *Psychological Review,* 108 (2001), 814–34.

23. P. Ebersole and K. DeVogler-Ebersole, "Meaning in Life of the

Eminent and the Average," *Journal of Social Behavior and Personality,* vol. 1, no. 1 (January 1985), 83–94. This study is especially interesting because it was testing a hypothesis put forth by the philosopher Will Durant, who had extensively studied eminent people through the ages.

24. A. Colby, L. Sippola, and E. Phelps, "Social Responsibility and Paid Work," in A. Rossi, ed., *Caring and Doing for Others: Social Responsibility in the Domains of Family, Work, and Community* (Chicago: University of Chicago Press, 2001).

25. Ibid., p. 86.

26. Ibid.

27. See Colby and Damon, *Some Do Care: Contemporary Lives of Moral Commitment.*

28. "A Church's Challenge: Holding On to Its Young," *New York Times,* January 16, 2007, p. 5.

29. "Religion's Generation Gap," *Wall Street Journal,* March 2, 2007, p. W1.

CHAPTER 3

1. The sites were, respectively: Trenton, New Jersey; Santa Clara County, California; a town in Tennessee; Fresno, California; and Stockton, California.

2. As noted in chapter 1, the quantitative results reported in this book draw largely from approximately fifty interviews and four hundred surveys that we conducted for the first wave of our study, completed in 2006. For a few of the analyses and examples I draw from the larger number of follow-up interviews

that we conducted in 2007, but as of this writing the bulk of these recent data have yet to be analyzed. Over the next few years, we shall be analyzing survey and interview data from our more recent studies, and will continue to collect substantial new data as well. We shall be reporting our next wave of findings in scientific journals over the next five to ten years.

3. All of the results reported in this chapter are approximations from the first round of studies, completed in 2006. The exact figures most likely will be modified as we analyze further data from studies we are continuing to conduct at present. As new and/or revised findings come in, we will report them in scientific and professional journals.

4. See N. Garmezy, "Stressors of Childhood," in N. Garmezy and M. Rutter, eds., *Stress, Coping, and Development in Children* (New York: McGraw-Hill, 1983).

5. Chris Hedges, "35% of High School Seniors Fail National Civics Test," *New York Times,* Sunday, November 21, 1999.

6. *The Civic and Political Health of the Nation: National Youth Survey of Civic Engagement 2002* (Center for Information and Research on Civic Learning and Engagement, University of Maryland, 2002).

7. Susan Verducci and William Damon, "The Outlooks of Today's Teens," in Richard Lerner and Jacqueline Lerner, eds., *Adolescents A to Z* (New York: Oxford University Press, 2000).

8. See Doug McAdam, *Freedom Summer* (Oxford: Oxford University Press, 1990).

9. One of the more memorable answers that I received to this puzzle was from the Dalai Lama, during a public "dialogue" I was invited to have with him in September 2006. After I pre-

sented my findings on youth purpose (the findings reported in this chapter), I was invited to ask one question. I chose the question of what to do about the kids who seemed to be wholly uninterested in finding purpose. He replied that the solution was to vividly impress upon these youngsters both the "downsides and upsides"—the benefits of finding moral purpose and the harms of purposelessness. The entire exchange can be found at http://ed.stanford.edu/suse/news-bureau/display Record.php?tablename=susenews&id=186.

10. "Report on the Official Account of the Bombings in London on 11 May 2006." House of Commons, Westminster, U.K.

11. The first quote is from the House of Commons Report, the second from the Wikipedia article on the bombings (http://en .wikipedia.org/wiki/July_7_bombings).

12. Reported in the *Denver Post,* July 7, 2006.

13. *Time* magazine, December 20, 1999, p. 42.

14. This, of course, is reminiscent of the maxim that many of us heard in childhood: "Idle hands are the devil's workshop." The educational value of maxims for social and moral learning is discussed in the last chapter.

CHAPTER 4

1. Anne Colby and I came to much the same conclusion in our study of moral exemplars, *Some Do Care: Contemporary Lives of Moral Commitment*. Although the twenty-three people we studied had accomplished many admirable things, the processes through which they acquired and sustained their

commitments were the same as those by which any person acquires a more normal range of moral habits and beliefs (such as refraining from harming others or caring for loved ones). In the case of the exemplars, the commitments were developed to heroic and far-reaching degrees, but the psychological and behavioral differences were in degree rather than in kind.

2. See William Damon and Richard Lerner, eds., *Handbook of Child Psychology,* 6th ed. (New York: John Wiley, 2006), esp. vols. 1 and 3.

3. Ibid., esp. vol. 3, chap. 6, by Avshalom Caspi.

4. In particular, Nina acknowledges the help of ACS staff members Beth Stevenson and Linelle Blais.

5. William Damon and Daniel Hart, *Self-Understanding in Childhood and Adolescence* (New York: Cambridge University Press, 1988).

6. Ibid.

7. Csikszentmihalyi, *Finding Flow,* p. 5.

8. K. Bronk, "Exemplars of Youth Purpose: A set of twelve case studies in adolescent commitment." Unpublished manuscript, Stanford University.

CHAPTER 5

1. A. Astin, "The Changing American College Student: 30 Year Trends, 1966–1996," *Review of Higher Education,* vol. 21, no. 2 (1998), 115–35. According to follow-up studies, the double trend that Astin and his colleagues observed—an increase in students' material goals combined with a decrease in their goals

related to life meaning—has continued gathering steam during the first decade of the twenty-first century.

2. For a trenchant critique of this and other related shortcomings of today's academic institutions, see D. Bok, *Our Underachieving Colleges* (Princeton, NJ: Princeton University Press, 2005).

3. The stream of unsavory material is incessant and unstoppable. After MySpace and Facebook cleaned up their acts with regard to sex and violence, a host of other widely viewed sites quickly arose in their place—see B. Stone, "Young Turn to Web Sites Without Rules," *New York Times,* January 2, 2007, p. 1.

4. See the JTF Web site (templetonfoundation.org) for more studies of purpose in the life sciences and cosmology.

5. R. Kiyosaki, *Rich Dad, Poor Dad: What the Rich Teach Their Kids About Money—and the Poor and Middle Class Do Not* (New York: Warner Books, 1997).

6. T. H. Eker, *Secrets of the Millionaire Mind* (New York: Harper-Collins, 2005).

7. R. Lieber, "Boiling Down Top Finance Books," *Wall Street Journal,* December 30, 2006, p. B1.

8. For an extended discussion of first causes and subsequent snowballing effects in youth development, see William Damon, *Social and Personality Development: Infancy Through Adolescence* (New York: W. W. Norton, 1983).

9. See William Damon, *The Moral Child* (New York: Free Press, 1992).

10. M. McPherson, L. Smith-Lovin, and M. Brashers, "Social Isolation in America: Changes in core discussion networks over two decades," *American Sociological Review,* 71 (2006), p. 371.

CHAPTER 6

1. Penelope Leach, *Children First: What Society Must Do—and Is Not Doing—for Children Today* (New York: Vintage Books, 1995).

2. The "Say Yes to No" Coalition, founded in Minnesota by psychologist David Walsh—see J. Zaslow, "The Entitlement Epidemic," *Wall Street Journal,* July 19, 2007, p. D1.

3. Peter Benson, *Sparks: How Parents Can Ignite the Hidden Strengths of Teenagers* (San Francisco: Jossey-Bass, 2008).

4. See Robert Emmons, *Thanks: The Psychology of Gratitude* (New York: HarperCollins, 2007).

5. See Damon, *Greater Expectations*.

6. Colby, Sippola, and Phelps, "Social Responsibility and Paid Work," in Rossi, ed., *Caring and Doing for Others: Social Responsibility in the Domains of Family, Work, and Community*.

7. Jared Sandberg, "To Our Kids, Our Jobs Are Talking, Typing. Are They Onto Us?" *Wall Street Journal,* June 17, 2007, p. B1.

8. See R. Whalen, *The Founding Father: The Story of Joseph P. Kennedy and His Political Dynasty* (Washington, DC: Regnery Gateway, 1964).

9. Ben Stein, "Getting a Boost Up the Ladder of Success," *New York Times,* Sunday, July 15, 2007, p. 6.

10. See R. Pianta, *Beyond the Parent* (San Francisco: Jossey-Bass, 1992).

11. See Mary Rothbart and J. Bates, "Temperament," in Damon, ed., *Handbook of Child Psychology,* 5th ed., pp. 105–77.

12. See, e.g., Martin Seligman, et al., *The Optimistic Child* (Boston:

Houghton Mifflin, 1995) and Carolyn Saarni, *The Development of Emotional Competence* (New York: Guilford, 1999).

CHAPTER 7

1. Thomas Mann, *The Magic Mountain* (November 1924, English trans. John E. Woods (New York: Everyman's Library/Knopf, 1995).
2. See Glen Elder, *Children of the Great Depression* (Chicago: University of Chicago Press, 1975).
3. For a fuller treatment of how exemplary people can influence others to turn a life of hardship into moral purpose, see Colby and Damon, *Some Do Care: Contemporary Lives of Moral Commitment.*
4. William Damon, *The Youth Charter: How Communities Can Work Together to Raise Standards for All Our Children* (New York: Free Press, 1997).
5. Richard Lerner, *The Good Teen* (New York: Random House, 2007).
6. NPR, *All Things Considered,* August 30, 2007. The monkey bar and dodgeball bans were intended to prevent physical injury. Apparently the prohibition on tag was put in place to avoid the possibility of harassment (among schoolchildren!), a phenomenon that deserves its own critical analysis in some other venue.
7. See S. Harter, "The Self," in Damon and Lerner, eds., *Handbook of Child Psychology,* 6th ed.
8. See Damon, *Greater Expectations.*
9. See Maria Shriver, *And One More Thing Before You Go* (New

York: Free Press, 2005), for several other valuable words of wisdom about guidance for young people.

10. Chester E. Finn, Jr., and Diane Ravitch, "Not by Geeks Alone," *Wall Street Journal,* Wednesday, August 8, 2007, p. 13.

11. Ibid.

12. Ibid.

13. James Youniss and Miranda Yates, *Community Service and Social Responsibility in Youth* (Chicago: University of Chicago Press, 1997).

14. See Damon, "To Not Fade Away: Restoring Civil Identity Among the Young," in D. Ravitch and J. Viteritti, eds., *Making Good Citizens: Education and Civil Society* (New Haven: Yale University Press, 2001), 122–41.

15. "How Patriotic Are We?" *AARP Bulletin,* vol. 47, no. 7. (July-August 2006), p. 3.

16. Anne Colby, et al., *Educating for Democracy: Preparing Undergraduates for Responsible Political Engagement* (San Francisco: Jossey-Bass, 2007).

17. Journalism professor and political blogger Jeff Jarvis, quoted in A. Goodnough, "Oh Everyone Knows That Except You," *New York Times,* Sunday, September 2, 2007, p. D1.

18. Gail Collins, "Men's Room Chronicles," *New York Times,* August 30, 2007, p. 24.

19. Developmental psychology long has recognized status as one of the main determinants of who a young person imitates—see Damon, *Social and Personality Development.*

20. Michael Medved, *Hollywood vs. America: Popular Culture and the War on Traditional Values* (New York: Free Press, 1994).

21. This is not pie-in-the-sky. I have had several gratifying experi-

ences conducting discussions with groups of public figures (including business leaders and sports stars) about their responsibilities to set admirable examples for young people. Sometimes, especially in the case of sports stars, they have not realized the extent of their own influence. But when it starts to dawn on them, I have seen them willingly, even eagerly, rise to the occasion. Most adults really do want to do the right thing by the younger generation.

ACKNOWLEDGMENTS

My first words of thanks go to Arthur Schwartz, who encouraged my studies in youth purpose from the start and who has been a true partner in shaping the ideas at the center of the project. In addition to Arthur's advice, the John Templeton Foundation has supported the project in a most beneficent way that has provided not only generous material support but also a welcome source of inspiration. I thank Sir John Templeton, John M. Templeton Jr., and Charles L. Harper, Jr., for the many insights they have given me over the years. The other superb organization that has provided this work with invaluable support is the Thrive Foundation for Youth, and I offer my warmest thanks to Bob and Dottie King and to Cynthia King-Guffey for all that the foundation has done to make possible this and other research that I have conducted in positive youth development. An early version of my discussion of development in Chapter 2 of this book was first posted in the "Thoughts on Thriving" section of the foundation's Web site (http://www.thrivefoundation.org). I also thank Pam King for her many excellent contributions to these research efforts and the entire King family for their friendship.

Over the past seven years, I have had the opportunity to discuss my progress on this project with an extraordinarily talented group of developmental scholars assembled at least twice a year by the Thrive Foundation for Youth. The scholars in the Forum on Thriving have included Peter Benson, Peter Scales, Linda Wagener, Jim Furrow, Pam King, Richard Lerner, and Duncan Campbell. I thank all of them for their feedback and many intellectual contributions to my understanding of youth purpose.

At Stanford, Kendall Cotton Bronk and Jenni Menon helped carry out the initial phase of the research, the findings on which most of the discussions in this book are based. Kendall also helped design the present phase of the project, which entails a further, expanded data collection, and she served as project manager for the first two years of this present phase. When Kendall left Stanford last year, for a faculty position at Ball State University, Seana Moran replaced her as project manager. I thank both Kendall and Seana for all their talents and dedication: this project has benefited greatly from their excellent work. I have also been fortunate to have had a number of absolutely outstanding research assistants, including Jennifer Menon Mariano (who conducted the survey analyses that I drew on in this book), Matt Andrews, Matt Burdick, David Yeager, Norma Arce, Amina Jones, Peter Osborn, Tanya Rose, Jim Siriani, Brian Edgar, Tim Reilly, Heather Malin, Sarah Miles, and Mollie Galloway. On the Stanford administrative front, Kathy Davis, Taru Fisher, Lisa Staton, and Elissa Hirsch have all provided skillful assistance on many occasions, and I greatly appreciate all their good help.

I wish to give special mention to Karen Rathman for all that she has done for the Youth Purpose Project. Karen has spearheaded our efforts to link with secondary schools and encourage teachers to introduce notions of purpose into the classroom, and she has done this with energy, imagination, and good judgment. Karen has been an irreplaceable part of our project team for the past three years, adding greatly to virtually every part of the project. Finally, I express my appreciation to my agent, Susan Arellano, and my editor, Emily Loose, each of whom have helped me immensely in the process of organizing my thoughts and conclusions into the present book, and I express my enduring thanks to Anne Colby for all her immeasurable contributions to this work.

INDEX

ABOUT THE AUTHOR

WILLIAM DAMON is one of the world's leading scholars of human development. He is professor of education and Director of the Center on Adolescence at Stanford University. Prior to coming to Stanford in 1997, Damon was University Professor and Director of the Center for the Study of Human Development at Brown University. He speaks regularly to public and academic groups about contemporary trends in child development, and he has written widely about personal development and moral commitment at all ages of life. His books include *The Moral Child, Some Do Care, Greater Expectations, The Youth Charter,* and *Good Work*. He is founding editor of the well-known series New Directions for Child and Adolescent Development and editor in chief of *The Handbook of Child Psychology,* 5th and 6th editions. Among other national recognitions, he was recently elected to the National Academy of Education. Damon lives in Northern California.